Obstetrics & Gynaecology Mcqs

NISHANT BHUSHAN

ABOUT THE AUTHOR

NISHANT BHUSHAN LIVES IN JAMSHEDPUR AND COMPLETED HIS 10TH FROM DAV BISTUPUR, FURTHER HE WENT TO SRI CHAITANIYA VIZAG FOR HIS HIGHER SECONDARY BOARDS AND FINALLY STARTED HIS JOURNEY BY PURSUING M.B.B.S FROM SRI LAKSHMI NARAYANA INSTITUTE OF MEDICAL SCIENCE PONDICHERRY.

FOR MORE DETAILS PLEASE VISIT OUR WEBSITE
www.nishantbhushan.in

PART-I

1. A 48-year-old woman presents with intermenstrual bleeding for two months and episodes of bleeding occurring any time in the cycle. There is no associated pain. Differential diagnosis for intermenstrual bleeding does not include:
a. endocervical polyp
b. cervical malignancy
c. endometrial polyp
d. ovarian teratoma
e. atrophic vaginitis.

Answer: d
3. All of the following are effects of premature menopause, apart from:
a. decreased cardiovascular risk
b. infertility
c. osteoporosis
d. vasomotor symptoms
e. vaginal dryness.

Answer: a
4. A 32-year-old woman presents to the gynaecology clinic with infrequent periods. A hormone profi le is done and all of the following are consistent with polycystic ovarian syndrome, apart
from:
a. increased androgen levels
b. normal FSH

c. normal oestradiol
d. decreased LH
e. low progesterone levels.

Answer: d
5. A 28-year-old woman attends the colposcopy clinic after an abnormal smear test. The smear is reported as severe dyskaryosis and she has an intrauterine contraceptive device in situ. All of the following statements are likely to be true, apart from:
a. the cervix is macroscopically normal
b. acetic acid is applied and an irregular white area is apparent to the left of the cervical os
c. Lugol's iodine is applied and the same area stains dark brown while the rest of the cervix stains pale
d. a biopsy is taken
e. the IUCD can stay, as it will not aggravate the cervical abnormality.

Answer: c
6. A 24-year-old woman presents with the absence of periods for nine months. She started her periods at the age of 13 years and had a regular 28-day cycle until 18 months ago. The periods then became irregular, occurring every two to three months until they stopped completely. The following are all included in the differential diagnosis of secondary amenorrhoea, apart from:
a. excessive exercise
b. hyperprolactinaemia
c. hyperthyroidism
d. premature ovarian failure
e. signifi cant weight loss

Answer: c
7. The following statements regarding adenomyosis are true, apart from one.

a. It tends to occur in women over 35 years.
b. Risk factors include increased parity, termination and quick labours.
c. The condition commonly occurs in association with endometriosis.
d. With each period, bleeding occurs from the endometrial tissue into the smooth muscle.
e. The diagnosis can be made by ultrasound or magnetic resonance imaging scan.

Answer: b

8. A 20-year-old woman is referred with a problem of post-coital bleeding. Over the past two months it has occurred on six occasions and there has been a small amount of bright red blood noticed after intercourse. There is no associated pain. The following investigations should initially be performed, apart from:

a. cervical smear
b. endocervical swab for chlamydia
c. colposcopy
d. endocervical swab for gonorrhoea
e. speculum examination to observe the cervix.

Answer: c

9 The following are all consistent with the diagnosis of antiphospholipid syndrome except:

a hydatidiform mole
b severe early-onset pre-eclampsia c arterial or venous thrombosis
d mid-trimester fetal loss e placental abruption.

Answer: a

10. The following are all causes of recurrent miscarriage, apart from:

a. parental chromosomal abnormality
b. activated protein C-resistance
c. uncontrolled hypothyroidism
d. chlamydia infection
e. submucosal fi broids.

Answer: d

11. Which one of the following statements about pituitary tumours is true?

a. Weight loss is a common feature of pituitary failure (hypopituitarism)

due to a pituitary tumour.

b. Visual fi eld loss in female patients with prolactin-secreting pituitary tumours (prolactinoma) is usual.
c. Adrenocorticotrophic hormone (ACTH) secreting pituitary tumours cause a syndrome of cortisol excess that can lead to exaggerated vertical growth in adolescence.
d. Growth hormone defi ciency is a recognised feature in adult patients presenting with acromegaly due to a pituitary macroadenoma.
e. A low testosterone level is more common than a low thyroxine level in men with non-functioning gonads.

Answer: e

12. Which of the following statements concerning the anterior pituitary is true?

a. It develops in the embryo from a down-growth of the hypothalamus.
b. It secretes antidiuretic hormone (ADH).
c. It is regulated by hypothalamic-releasing hormones.
d. It secretes its hormones into the pituitary portal system.
e. It is down-regulated by low oestrogen levels.

Answer: c

13. Which one of the following statements about the implantation of the human embryo is true?

a. It will occur at any time over a period of about 14 days.
b. It will occur whether or not the zona pellucida is present.
c. It will occur when the cytotrophoblast contacts the endometrial epithelium and begins to invade the maternal

tissue.
d. It will occur with the inner cell mass closest to the endometrium.
e. It will occur even if there is only cytotrophoblast present.

Answer: d
14. Which one of the following statements about puberty is true?
a. Puberty is preceded by falling plasma levels of adrenal androgens.
b. The fi rst menstrual period is called the adrenarche.
c. The pubertal growth spurt is the fi rst sign of puberty.
d. Pubic hair growth is stimulated in girls by oestrogen.
e. Spermatogenesis starts at puberty.

Answer: a
15. Which is the most appropriate statement concerning pulmonary embolism?
a. It is now rarely fatal, with the introduction of modern diagnostic tests and treatments.
b. It gives an area of lung which is unventilated on a ventilationperfusion

scan.
c. It does not usually show up on a CT pulmonary angiogram.
d. It is likely that the patient has symptoms of deep-vein thrombosis.
e. It may give symptoms similar to pneumonia.

Answer: e
16. One of the following is true. It is recognised that the positive predictive value of initial mammography for breast cancer within the national screening programme in the UK is 16%. This means that:
a. 16% of people who have breast cancer are detected on initial mammography
b. 84% of people without breast cancer have a normal mammogram
c. 16% of initial mammograms are abnormal
d. a patient with an abnormal initial mammogram has a 16% chance of having breast cancer
e. out of every 100 patients with an abnormal mammogram,

Answer: d
17. One of the following is true. Successful fertilisation and subsequent normal embryonic development:
a. require at least two spermatozoa
b. require the retention of the cortical granules in the oocyte
c. are most likely when the oocytes have been ovulated in an immature stage
d. require exclusion of the second polar body
e. often occur when the oocyte has lost its zona pellucida.

Answer: d
18. One of the following is true. The increase in maternal blood volume in pregnancy occurs as a result of:
a. peripheral vasoconstriction
b. a reduction in progesterone
c. decreased synthesis of vasopressin
d. increased aldosterone synthesis
e. reduced renin activity.

Answer: d

19. One of the following is true. Decreased peripheral resistance in pregnancy has been attributed to an increase in synthesis of:
a. angiotensin
b. endothelin
c. nitric oxide

d. renin
e. thromboxane.
Answer: c
20. A 25-year-old woman on liver enzyme inducers is requesting contraceptive advice. The method providing her with the most reliable form of contraception would be:
a. combined oral contraceptive pill
b. Depo-Provera injection
c. diaphragm
d. male condom
e. progesterone-only pill.

Answer: b
21. A 35-year-old woman comes requesting long-term reversible contraception. You advise that the method that can provide the longest protection is:
a. contraceptive implant
b. copper intrauterine device
c. Depo-Provera injection
d. intrauterine hormonal system (IUS)
e. laparoscopic sterilisation.

Answer: b
22. Regarding cervical cancer, which is the true statement?
a. HPV types 6 and 12 are high risk for developing cervical cancer.
b. The new vaccines can prevent invasive carcinoma but not CIN.
c. As soon as the new vaccination is introduced, cervical screening programmes can cease.
d. HPV types 16 and 18 account for the majority of cervical cancer in the UK.
e. HPV is an oncogenic virus for squamous cell but not adenocarcinoma of the cervix.

Answer: d
23. Regarding the menstrual cycle, which is the true statement?
a. Menstruation occurs with vasodilation of the spiral arteries.
b. The LH surge triggers menstruation.
c. The Graafi an follicle develops during the luteal phase.
d. Both the follicle and the corpus luteum secrete oestradiol.
e. Progesterone levels fall after the onset of menstruation.

Answer: d
24. Regarding Müllerian duct abnormalities which is the true statement?

a. occur about 1 in 500
b. the commonest uterine abnormality is septate uterus
c. occur not infrequently with gastrointestinal abnormalities
d. surgical correction of a septate uterus is followed by fetal salvage in

<60% of cases
e. longitudinal vaginal septa are more common than transverseones.

Answer: b
25. Choose the correct statement: Uterine leiomyosarcomas:

a. are associated with exposure to tamoxifen
b. originate from leiomyomas
c. pelvic radiotherapy has a signifi cant impact on survival
d. commonly metastasise to the brain
e. anthracycline-based chemotherapy has no place in treatment.

Answer: a
GYNAECOLOGY Objective type Questions with Answers
26. Which one of the following statements about the menopause is correct?
a. Progesterone levels rise after the menopause.
b. LH levels rise after the menopause.
c. The pituitary stops secreting LH and FSH at the menopause.
d. Menstrual cycles remain regular until the last menstrual period.
e. The number of oocytes in the ovary remains constant until the menopause.

Answer: b
27. Choose the correct statement: The female reproductive tract plays important roles in sperm transport by:
a. trapping most spermatozoa in the cervical crypt for many days
b. regulating sperm transport so that cells reach the site of fertilisation around the time of ovulation
c. allowing sperm transport at all stages of the ovarian cycle
d. preventing spermatozoa from swimming out of the peritoneal cavity
e. providing an acidic environment to keep the spermatozoa active.

Answer: b
28. Which one of the following statements is true: Semen analysis:
a. identifi es men with high-quality fertile spermatozoa
b. identifi es men with low sperm concentrations that might affect fertility
c. can always be used to predict fertility
d. cannot identify abnormal spermatozoa

e. identifi es men with hypopituitarism.

Answer: b
29. One of the following is true. A malignant tumour arising in the mesenchymal tissue is called:
a. adenoma
b. carcinoma
c. lymphoma
d. melanoma
e. sarcoma.

Answer: e
30. One of the following is true. Affording moral status to a human embryo/fetus means that it now has:
a. an inalienable right to life
b. a right to life
c. a right to consideration
d. a right dependent on moral consensus
e. a right not to be harmed.

Answer: d
31. At term amniotic fluid volume is
a. 800ml
b. 500 ml

c. 400 ml
d. 600 ml

Answer: a
32. what is the principal carbohydrate present in Amniotic fluid ?
a. Glucose
b. Fructose
c. Mannose
d. Galactose

Answer: a
33. Oligohydramnios is related which of the following condition ?
a. Renal Agenesis
b. esophageal atresia
c. anencephaly
d. down's syndrome

Answer: a
34. Early amniocentesis is done in which period of pregnancy
a. 12-14 wks
b. 14-16 wks
c. 16-18 wks
d. 9-11 wks

Answer: b
35. Immune rejection of fetus prevented by
a. HCG
b. HPL
c. oestrogen
d. progesterone

Answer: a
36. what happens to GFR in a case of Pre-eclampsia ?
a. GFR Decreases
b. GFR increases
c. remains same
d. none of the above

Answer: a
37. Shortest diameter of pelvic Cavity
a. Interspinous
b. transverse
c. antero-posterior
d. oblique

Answer: a
38. Large Chorioangioma associated with
a. polyhydroamnios
b. oligohydramnios
c. both
d. none

Answer: a
39. Commonest presentation of Choriocarcinoma

a. vaginal bleeding
b. abdominal pain
c. breathlessness
d. perforation of the uterus

Answer: a
40. Frog eye appearance is seen in
a. Anencephaly

b. acardia
c. down's syndrome
d. patau's syndrome

Answer: a
41. what of the following is seen in Partial mole
a. Triploidy
b. haploidy
c. polyploidy
d. diploidy

Answer: a
42. Cervical changes in pregnancy are all except ?
a. increased collagen
b. increased Hyaluronic acid
c. Increased glands
d. increased vascularity

Answer: b
GYNAECOLOGY Questions and Answers pdf Download
1. Women with postmenopausal bleeding need endometrial sampling if endometrial on US is thicker than
A. 1mm

B. 2mm

C. 5mm

D. 8mm

E. 10mm

Answer: C.5mm
2. Which of the following change in puberty is influenced by the estrogen:
A. Growth of the acinar buds of the breast

B. Epiphyseal fusion

C. Proliferatve phase

D. All of the above

E. None of the above

Answer: D.All of the above
3. not exclusevely in the stomach121. Pelvic ultrasound is helpful in the diagnosis of:

A. Endometrial carcinoma

B. Asherman's syndrome

C. Ascites

D. Ovulation detection

E. Endometriosis

Answer: D.Ovulation detection

4. Glycogen is seen in the lumina of endometrial glands :

A. During the luteal phase

B. During pregnancy only

C. During pre and post ovulatory

D. During proliferative phase only

E. At the time of ovulation only

Answer: A.During the luteal phase

5. The Wolfian duct in the female :

A. Develops into the fallopian tube

B. Forms the ovary

C. Forms the round ligament

D. Regresses and becomes vestigial

E. None of the above

Answer: D.Regresses and becomes vestigial

6. Large amount of alkaline phosphatase may be demonstrated in the endometrium of :

A. Decidua

B. Secretory phase

C. Proliferative phase

D. All of the above

E. None of the above

Answer: C.Proliferative phase

7. Oxytocin and vasopressin are transferred from hypothalamus to neurohypophysis through:

A. Venous channels

B. Lymphatics

C. Nerve axons

D. All of the above

E. None of the above

Answer: C.Nerve axons
8. The levator ani muscle :
A. Is a voluntary muscle

B. Is attached laterally to the "white line of the pelvis "

C. Is composed of pubococcygeus and iliococcygeus muscle

D. Contracts to prevent spillage of urine during strain

E. All of the above

Answer: E.All of the above
9. The function of round ligament is :
A. Vestigial with no apparent function

B. To prevent retrodisplacement of the uterus

C. To prevent uterine prolapse

D. To provide nerve supply of the upper vagina

E. None of the above

Answer: B.To prevent retrodisplacement of the uterus
10. The definitive epithelium of vagina is derived from :
A. Wolfian duct

B. Mullerian duct

C. Urogenital epithelium

D. Coelomic epithelium

E. none

Answer: C.Urogenital epithelium
11. Causes of post partum amenorrhoea may be :
A. Anorexia nervosa

B. Cervical atresia

C. Chlorpromazaine therapy

D. Any of the above

E. None of the above

Answer: D.Any of the above
12. The cyclic production of pituitary hormones is dependant upon:
A. Normal menstruation

B. An intact pituitary- portal system

C. An adult anterior pituitary gland

D. All of the above

E. None of the above

Answer: B.An intact pituitary- portal system

13. The clots passed with menorrhagia perhaps indicate

A. No endometrial regeneration

B. No terminal arteriolar spasm

C. Large amount of bleeding

D. All of the above

E. None of the above

Answer: C.Large amount of bleeding

14. Monilial vagintis occurs frquently during pregnancy because :

A. Glycosuria is commoner

B. The vagina contains more glycogen

C. Higher vaginal acidity suppresses other organisms

D. All of the above

E. None of the above

Answer: D.All of the above

15. Physical exam reveals the uterus to be about 6 wk size. Vaginal bleeding is scanty with no discernible tissue in the cervical os. There are no palpable adnexal masses. The uterus is mildly tender. Ultrasonographic exam does not reveal a gestational sac. Which of the following should be recommended?

A. Dilatation & curettage.

B. Culdocentesis.

C. Observation followed by serial B-HCG determinations.

D. Diagnostic laparoscopy.

E. Laparotomy

Answer: D.Diagnostic laparoscopy.

16. Which of the following statements Is incorrect regarding levonorgestrel releasing intrauterine system:

A. There is increased incidence of menorrhagia

B. This system can be used as hormone replacement therapy

C. This method is useful for the treatment of endometerial hyperplasia

D. Irregular uterine bleeding can be problem initially

E. none

Answer: A.There is increased incidence of menorrhagia
17. Myxoma peritonei may occur as a consequence of rupture of which ovarian cyst ?
A. Dermoid

B. Struma ovarii

C. Serous cystadenoma

D. Mucinous cystadenoma

E. Cystadenofibroma

Answer: D.Mucinous cystadenoma
18. Lutein and theca lutein cysts may be associated with all the following except :
A. Mole

B. Chorionepithelioma

C. Stein-leventhal syndrome(PCO)

D. Pregnancy

E. Abortion

Answer: C.Stein-leventhal syndrome(PCO)
19. The site of primary infection in patients with pelvic tuberculosis is usually
A. Tubal

B. Uterine

C. Cervical

D. Ovarian

E. Lungs

Answer: E.Lungs
20. The preferred treatment of ruptured tubo-ovarian abscess is
:
A. Cul-de-sac drainage

B. Removal of uterus , tubes and involved ovary

C. Removal of uterus , tubes and ovaries

D. Removal of ruptured tube and ovary

E. Removal of adenexae and drainage

Answer: C.Removal of uterus , tubes and ovaries
21. The cysts of Stein -Leventhal ovary or PCOD are of which kind?
A. Lutein

B. Germinal inclusion

C. Follicular

D. Theca lutein

E. Endometrial

Answer: C.Follicular
22. Clinical findings of PCOD include all except :
A. Obesity

B. Olgomenorrhoea

C. Infertility

D. Tall stature

E. none

Answer: D.Tall stature
23. Pyogenic infections of genital tract usually spread via :
A. Mucous membrane

B. Veins

C. Lymphatics

D. Fistulous tracts

E. B+C

Answer: E.B+C
24. Presence of pyometra in a post menopausal females strongly suggests:
A. Diabetes mellitus

B. Degenerating myoma

C. Senile endometritis

D. Malignancy

E. Sexual promiscuity

Answer: D.Malignancy
25. The most common symptom associated with adenomyosis is
:

A. Infertility

B. Menorrhagia

C. Haematometra

D. Dyspareunia

E. Metrorrhagia

Answer: B.Menorrhagia
26. Adenomyosis is often associated with all of the following except :
A. Endometrial hyperplasia

B. Myoma

C. Endometriosis

D. Mymetrial hypertrophy

E. Subinvolution of uterus

Answer: E.Subinvolution of uterus
27. Medadteam.org More than you dream125. A 63 old lady presents with abdominal mass & weight loss , was diagnosed as having an ovarian tumor , the most common ovarian tumour in this woman would be...:
A. epithelial tumour

B. germ cell tumour

C. stromal tumour

D. sex cord tumour

E. trophoblastic tumour

Answer: A.epithelial tumour
28. There is a 5% incidence of primary extrauterine malignancy associated with endometrial cancer, the most frequent site for such is :
A. Stomach

B. lung

C. Breast

D. Bone

E. Spleen

Answer: C.Breast
29. The cause of virilizing adrenal hyperplasia is :
A. Defect in cortisol synthesis

B. defect in ACTH synthesis

C. Defect in testosterone synthesis

D. All of the above

E. None of the above

Answer: A.Defect in cortisol synthesis
30. Anterior pituitary function may be blocked by:
A. Blood levels of steroids

B. Emotional factors

C. Sensory stimuli

D. All of the above

E. None of the above

Answer: D.All of the above
31. Subnuclear vaculoes in the endometrial mucosa are evidence of activity of:
A. Cholesterol
B. Progesterone

C. Pregnendiol

D. Androstenendione

E. Oestrogen

Answer: B.Progesterone
32. Common ovulation induced drugs are
A. Clomiphene citrate

B. Tamoxifen or the newer letrozole

C. Gonadotrophins

D. GnRh analogue down regulation protocols

E. All of the above

Answer: E.All of the above
33. The commonest cause of death in cancer cervix is :
A. Infection

B. Uraemia

C. Haemorrhage

D. Cachexia

E. Distant metastasis

Answer: B.Uraemia
34. Failure to find sperm in postcoital examination may be due to :
A. Excessive oestrogen effect on cervical mucous

B. Excessive vaginal lactic acid

C. Oligospermia

D. All of the above

E. None of the above

Answer: C.Oligospermia
35. The differential diagnosis of vaginal cysts include :
A. Cystocele

B. Urethral diverticulum

C. Urethrocoele

D. All of the above

E. None of the above

Answer: D.All of the above
36. Factors in cervical cancer development EXCEPT:
A. HIV infection

B. Chlamydia infection

C. Breast cancer

D. Smoking

E. Immunosuppression

Answer: C.Breast cancer
37. A synthetic progestin. What is the most likely explanation for the contraceptive action of this drug?
A. Replacement of the LH surge by an FSH surge.

B. Abolition of the LH surge

C. Enhanced positive feedback of the hypothalamic-pituitary-gonadal axis.

D. Increased conversion of testosterone to estradiol.

E. Inadequate decidualization of the uterus.

Answer: E.Inadequate decidualization of the uterus.
38. All of the following mechanisms might account for a reduced risk of upper genitaltract infection in users of progestin releasing IUDs, except:
A. Reduced retrograde menstruation
B. Decreased ovulation

C. Thickened cervical mucus

D. Decidual changes in the endometrium

E. All of the above

Answer: E.All of the above
39. Non-neoplastic ovarian cysts include all of the following except:
A. follicular cyst

B. theca lutein cyst

C. dermoid cyst

D. corpus luteum cyst

E. endmetroid cyst

Answer: C.dermoid cyst
40. Which of the following ovarian tumor is most prone to undergo torsion duringpregnancy?
A. Serous cystadenoma

B. Mucinous cystadenoma

C. Dermoid cyst

D. Theca lutein cyst

E. none

Answer: C.Dermoid cyst
41. Magnesium sulphate toxicity include all EXCEPT;
A. CNS depression

B. This drug acts only on motor end plate

C. Respiratory depression

D. muscle relaxant

E. none

Answer: B.This drug acts only on motor end plate

42. In DUB all are right except,:
A. may be associated with hypothyroidism

B. may be associated with post-menopausal bleeding

C. may be associated with functional ovarian cysts

D. may present as menorrhagia

E. may be present as metropathia hemorrhagica

Answer: B.may be associated with post-menopausal bleeding
43. Metabolic causes of anovulatory DUB include all except :
A. Hypothyroidism

B. Halban's syndrome

C. Cushing's syndrome

D. Hyperthyroidism

E. diabetes mellitus

Answer: B.Halban's syndrome
44. The primary drainage of the lower vagina is to :
A. external iliac nodes

B. Sacral nodes

C. Femoral nodes

D. superficial inguinal nodes

E. internal iliac nodes

Answer: D.superficial inguinal nodes
45. The most common causative organism in acute bartholinitis is
A. Staphylococcus

B. Streptococcus

C. Colon bacillus
D. Gonococcus

E. Trichomonas

Answer: D.Gonococcus
46. The uterine artery supplies the
A. Vagina

B. Lower cevix

C. Ovary

D. All of the above

E. None of the above

Answer: D.All of the above
47. Common accompaniments salpingitis are :
A. Pelvic mass

B. Bleeding

C. Pain

D. All of the above

E. None of the above

Answer: C.Pain
48. he ovary of new born may contain :

A. Small folicular cysts

B. Corpora lutea

C. Lutenized grnulosa cells

D. All of the above

E. None of the above

Answer: E.None of the above
49. Cervical amputation :
A. Is followed frequently by abortion
B. Is associated with high incidence of post operative sterility

C. Is not frequently followed by cervical dystocia in patients who become pregnant

D. All of the above

E. None of the above

Answer: D.All of the above
50. The effect of ovarian steroid on anterior pituitary is
A. Direct stimulation

B. Direct inhibition

C. Mediated via hypothalamus

D. Unknown

E. Direct stimulation and inhibition

Answer: C.Mediated via hypothalamus
51. What are the signs of ovulation on Ultrasonography :
A. Irregular follicle wall

B. Collapse of follicle

C. Fluid in cul de sac

D. All of the above

E. None of the above

Answer: D.All of the above
52. The uterus is held in anteflexed position by :
A. The ventral pull of round ligament

B. The dorsal pull of uterosacral ligaments

C. Its weight

D. All of the above

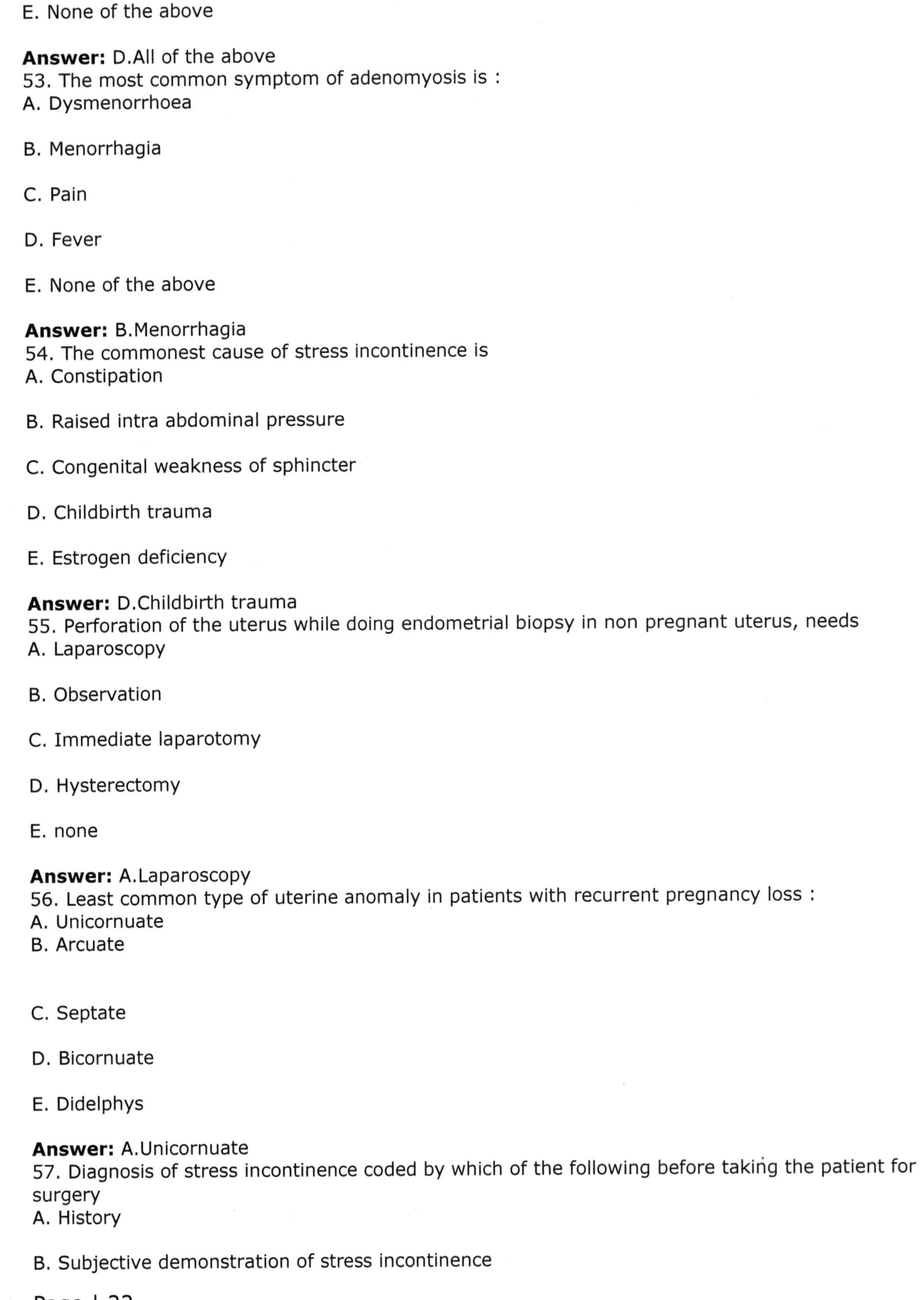

E. None of the above

Answer: D.All of the above
53. The most common symptom of adenomyosis is :
A. Dysmenorrhoea

B. Menorrhagia

C. Pain

D. Fever

E. None of the above

Answer: B.Menorrhagia
54. The commonest cause of stress incontinence is
A. Constipation

B. Raised intra abdominal pressure

C. Congenital weakness of sphincter

D. Childbirth trauma

E. Estrogen deficiency

Answer: D.Childbirth trauma
55. Perforation of the uterus while doing endometrial biopsy in non pregnant uterus, needs
A. Laparoscopy

B. Observation

C. Immediate laparotomy

D. Hysterectomy

E. none

Answer: A.Laparoscopy
56. Least common type of uterine anomaly in patients with recurrent pregnancy loss :
A. Unicornuate
B. Arcuate

C. Septate

D. Bicornuate

E. Didelphys

Answer: A.Unicornuate
57. Diagnosis of stress incontinence coded by which of the following before taking the patient for surgery
A. History

B. Subjective demonstration of stress incontinence

C. Objective demonstration of stress incontinence

D. Urodynamic studies

E. none

Answer: D.Urodynamic studies
58. The following are the factors associated with CIN EXCEPT
A. Onset of coitus at early stage

B. Multiple sexual partners

C. Lower socioeconomic status

D. Nulliparity

E. H/o veneral disease

Answer: D.Nulliparity
59. Best treatment for severe stress incontinence without prolapse is
A. Pelvic floor exercise

B. Kelly's repair

C. Burch colposuspension

D. MMK operation

E. Urethral collagen implant

Answer: B.Kelly's repair
60. Bartholin's gland duct opens in.....
A. Upper third of labia majora

B. Middle third of labia majora

C. Upper third of labia minora

D. Middle third of labia minora

E. none

Answer: D.Middle third of labia minora
61. A 19-year-old female comes to the physician because of left lower quadrant pain for 2 months. She states that she first noticed the pain 2 months ago but now it seems to be growing worse. She has had no changes in bowel or bladder function. She has no fevers or chills and no nausea, vomiting, or diarrhea. The pain is intermittent and sometimes feels like a dull pressure. Pelvic examination is significant for a left adnexal mass that is mildly tender. Urine hCG is negative. Pelvic ultrasound shows a 6 cm complex left adnexal mass with features consistent with a benign cystic teratoma (dermoid). Which of the following is the most appropriate next step in management?
A. Repeat pelvic examination in 1 year

B. Repeat pelvic ultrasound in 6 weeks

C. Prescribe the oral contraceptive pill

D. Perform hysteroscopy

E. perform laparotomy

Answer: E.perform laparotomy
62. A 54-year-old woman comes to the physician for an annual examination. She has no complaints. For the past year, she has been taking tamoxifen for the prevention of breast cancer. She was started on this drug after her physician determined her to be at high risk on the basis of her strong family history, nulliparity, and early age at menarche. She takes no other medications. Examination is within normal limits. Which of the following is this patient most likely to develop while taking tamoxifen?
A. Breast cancer
B. Elevated LDL cholesterol

C. Endometrial changes

D. Myocardial infarction

E. Osteoporosis

Answer: C.Endometrial changes
63. A 62-year-old woman comes to the physician because of bleeding from the vagina. She states that her last menstrual period came 11 years ago and that she has had no bleeding since that time. She has hypertension and type 2 diabetes mellitus. Examination shows a mildly obese woman in no apparent distress. Pelvic examination is unremarkable. An endometrial biopsy is performed that shows grade I endometrial adenocarcinoma. Which of the following is the most appropriate next step in management?
A. Chemotherapy

B. Cone biopsy

C. Dilation and curettage

D. Hysteroscopy

E. Hysterectomy

Answer: E.Hysterectomy
64. Ovarian precursors of oestradiol include :
A. Oestrone

B. Androstenedione

C. Testosterone

D. All of the above

E. None of the above

Answer: D.All of the above
65. Female patient with endometrial hyperplasia could be all of these except:
A. thecoma

B. fibroma

C. Brenner tumor

D. follicular cyst

E. none

Answer: B.fibroma
66. Endometroid cyst, on examination:
A. adenexal tenderness

B. cyst felt in thin people

C. cyst fixed and tender

D. all of the above .

E. none

Answer: D.all of the above .
67. Considering epithelial neoplasm of the ovaries all true except :
A. the commonest

B. mucinous cystadenoma lined by tubal epithelium

C. Brenner tumor lined by urinary tract epithelium

D. embryologically arise from wolffian epithelium .

E. none

Answer: B.mucinous cystadenoma lined by tubal epithelium
68. The Commonest ovarian neoplasm complicated with torsion during pregnancy:
A. fibroma

B. teratoma

C. simple serous cyst

D. thecoma .

E. none

Answer: B.teratoma
69. Female patient with acute abdomen , CBC normal , B-HCG negative , No vaginal bleeding , Mostly is :
A. hemorrhagic teratoma

B. disturbed ectopic pregnancy

C. appendicitis

D. peritonitis .

E. none

Answer: A.hemorrhagic teratoma
70. Considering mucinous cystadenoma :
A. the commonest neoplasm

B. usually bilateral

C. sometimes fill the entire abdominal cavity

D. lined by tubal epithelium .

E. none

Answer: C.sometimes fill the entire abdominal cavity
71. Considering Brenner tumor all true except :
A. potential malignant is common

B. histologically has epithelial nests and coffe bean nuclei

C. vaginal bleeding reported with it

D. usually in childbearing women

E. none

Answer: D.usually in childbearing women
72. Considering Meig's syndrome it is associated with :
A. ovarian fibroma

B. left side pleural effusion

C. ascitis

D. a&b

E. a&c

Answer: E.a&c
73. Considering malignant ovarian neoplasm histologically may be all except :
A. epithelial tumors

B. germ cells tumor

C. cystic and solid tumors

D. sex cord tumors .

E. none

Answer: C.cystic and solid tumors
74. For endometrial cyst all true except :
A. choclate cyst on TVS

B. laparoscope is indicated

C. C125 is a specific test

D. associated with dysmenoorrhoea .

E. none

Answer: C.C125 is a specific test
75. Female patient with history of induction of ovulation present with tender lowerabdominal pain and discomfort , TVS show cyst , Next step is :
A. assurance sending home

B. hold ovarian stimulatin drug

C. laparotomy

D. non of the above .

E. none

Answer: B.hold ovarian stimulatin drug
76. Considering endometroid cyst :
A. not uncommon

B. due to menstrual reaction

C. torsion is common

D. a&b .

E. all the above

Answer: D.a&b .
77. Considering endometrial cyst ttt all true except :
A. GNRH is of benefit

B. laparosope idicated in small cyst

C. laparotomy is preferred

D. recurrence is not common

E. none

Answer: D.recurrence is not common
78. Considering the follicular cyst it is rarely associated with :
A. endometrial hyperplasia

B. acute abdomen

C. polycystic ovary

D. On PV in obese patient it may rupture .

E. none

Answer: B.acute abdomen

79. Female patient with history of endometriosis , menstrual disorders complaining from pain on right iliac fossa , on examination there was tenderness on right iliac fossa with no rebound pain no rigidity , on CBC it was normal , most likely :
A. peritonitis

B. appendicitis

C. follicular cyst

D. non of the above

E. none

Answer: C.follicular cyst
80. Considering a case of follicular cyst it need all of following except :
A. assurance follow up

B. OCP

C. usually surgical removal

D. repeated US

E. none

Answer: C.usually surgical removal
81. Considering the follicular cyst all of following is true except :
A. associated with metropathia hemorrhagica

B. OCP indicated in ttt

C. the second common functional cyst

D. TAS is the gold standard diagnostic method

E. none

Answer: C.the second common functional cyst
82. Considering the endometroid cyst :
A. associated with dysmenorrhoea

B. associated with pelvic pain

C. associatd with pelvic endometriosis

D. All of the above
E. none

Answer: D.All of the above
83. Female patient with history of hydatiform and complaining of lower abdominal pain , on examination there was tenderness on palpation and the lab result show high level of HCG , most likely to be :
A. follicular cyst

B. theca lutein cyst

C. corpus luteum cyst

D. none of the above .

E. all

Answer: B.theca lutein cyst
84. A 29-year-old G4P4 is found to have an abnormal smear signed out as atypical glandular cells, favouring neoplasia. She undergoes a colposcopy with cervical biopsies. One of the ectocervical biopsies demonstrated adenocarcinima in the situ. The most appropriate next step is:
A. Vaginal hysterectomy

B. Radical hysterectomy/Radiotherapy

C. Cold-knife conization of the cervix

D. Loop excision of the cervical tranformation zone

E. none

Answer: C.Cold-knife conization of the cervix
85. The following about human papilloma virus (HPV) infection are correct EXCEPT:
A. It is the most common viral STDs.

B. It may lead CIN and cervical cancer.

C. It is due to RNA virus.

D. Infection may be warty or flat condyloma.

E. Infection is usually associated with others STDs.

Answer: C.It is due to RNA virus.
86. The lymphatic drainage of the cervix is to the following lymph nodes EXCEPT:
A. The femoral lymph nodes.

B. The internal iliac lymph nodes.

C. The para-cervical lymph nodes.

D. The pre-sacral lymh nodes.

E. The Obturator lymph nodes

Answer: A.The femoral lymph nodes.
87. The commonest secondary change in uterine fibroids is:
A. Fatty degeneration

B. Myxomatous degeneration.

C. Hyaline degeneration

D. Cystic degeneration

E. Calcification

Answer: C.Hyaline degeneration
88. The following is correct about the ovarian ligaments:
A. Contain ureters.

B. Contain ovarian arteries.

C. Are attached laterally to pelvic wall.

D. Lie anterior to the broad ligament.

E. Are homologous to part of the gubernaculums testis in the male

Answer: B.Contain ovarian arteries.
89. The severity of CIN is graded A. 1-3

B. 1a-4a

C. I-III+ I-IV

D. A-C

E. none

Answer: A.1-3
90. Cervical polyps
A. causes spontaneous abortion

B. are cause of antepartum hge

C. cause watery vaginal discharge

D. are covered by squamous epithelium

E. cause intermenstrual bleeding

Answer: E.cause intermenstrual bleeding
91. Involves pelvic LN clearance, hysterectomy, removal of the parametrium and theupper third of the vagina.
A. Wartman's hysterectomy

B. Wertheim's hysterectomy

C. Wertheims Trachelectomy

D. Radical trachelectomy

E. Trachelems hysterectomy

Answer: B.Wertheim's hysterectomy
92. 5 year survival for someone with stage 3-4 cervical carcinoma A. 10-30%!!!

B. 80-95%
C. 2-10%
D. 65-80%

E. 45-60%

Answer: A.10-30%!!!

93. Cervical carcinoma spread and staging: Microinvasion of the basement membrane, <7mm across, with no lymph/vascular space invasion

A. Stage 1b

B. Stage 3

C. Stage 4

D. Stage 1a

E. Stage 2a

Answer: D.Stage 1a

94. Acetic acid turns a portion of the cervix in a patient with a CIN

A. Green

B. Blue

C. Brown

D. Orange

E. White

Answer: E.White

95. Typical cells are found only in the lower third of the epithelium

A. CIN III

B. CIN I

C. CIN V

D. CIN IV

E. CIN II

Answer: E.CIN II

96. A 42-year-old G4P4 has had postcoital bleeding for the past four months. She has not had a Pap test since the delivery of her last child 7 years ago. Speculum examination shows a vaginal discharge and a 1 cm exophytic lesion of the posterior cervical lip. The most appropriate next

step is:

A. Perform a Pap smear

B. Perform a cold-knife conization

C. Give the patient a course of intravaginal Metronidazole gel followed by reexamination in 6 weeks

D. Perform a punch biopsy of the lesion

E. none

Answer: D.Perform a punch biopsy of the lesion

97. The area where cervical carcinoma usually originates

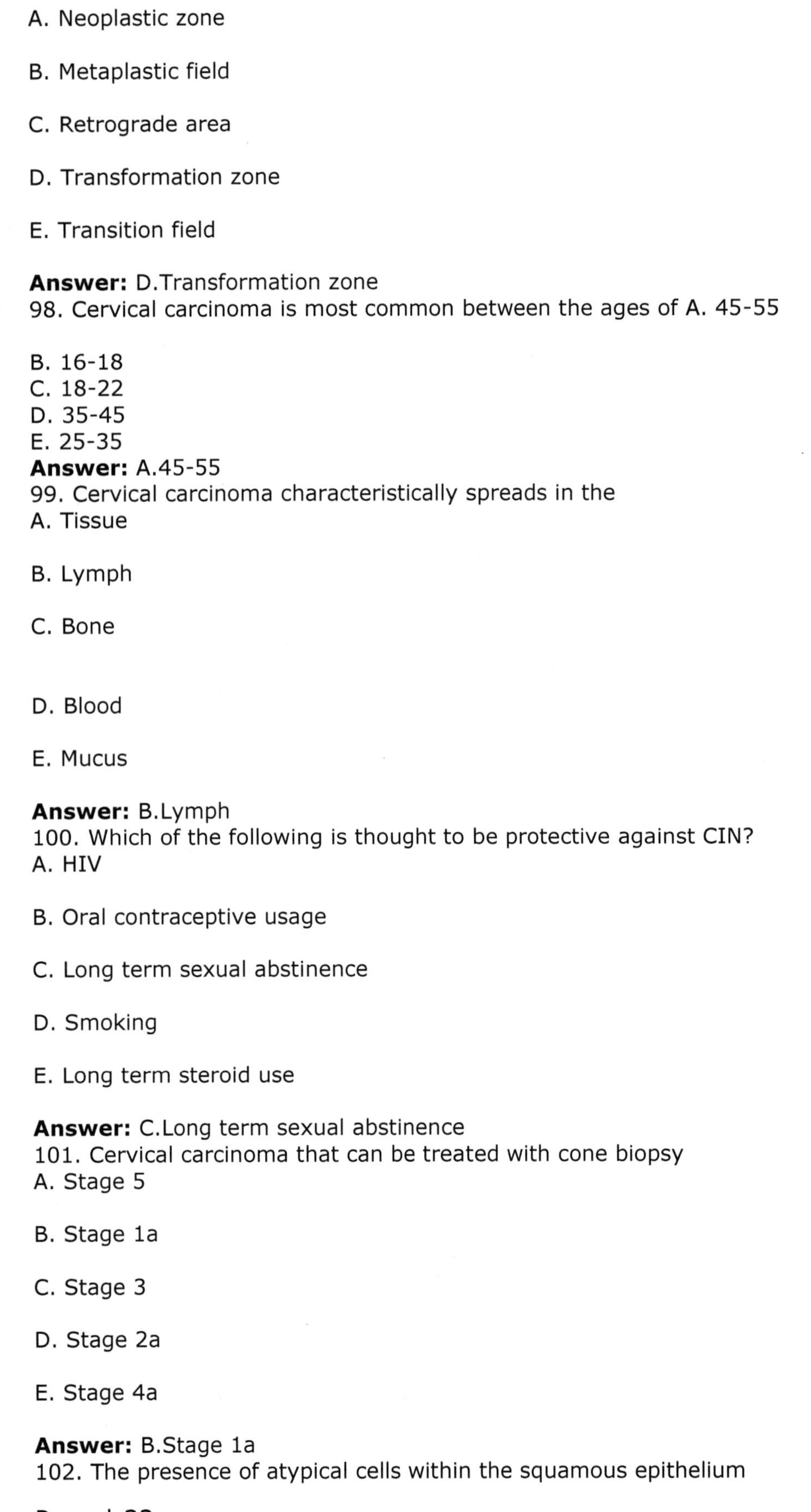

A. Neoplastic zone

B. Metaplastic field

C. Retrograde area

D. Transformation zone

E. Transition field

Answer: D.Transformation zone
98. Cervical carcinoma is most common between the ages of A. 45-55

B. 16-18
C. 18-22
D. 35-45
E. 25-35
Answer: A.45-55
99. Cervical carcinoma characteristically spreads in the
A. Tissue

B. Lymph

C. Bone

D. Blood

E. Mucus

Answer: B.Lymph
100. Which of the following is thought to be protective against CIN?
A. HIV

B. Oral contraceptive usage

C. Long term sexual abstinence

D. Smoking

E. Long term steroid use

Answer: C.Long term sexual abstinence
101. Cervical carcinoma that can be treated with cone biopsy
A. Stage 5

B. Stage 1a

C. Stage 3

D. Stage 2a

E. Stage 4a

Answer: B.Stage 1a
102. The presence of atypical cells within the squamous epithelium

A. Cervical dyskaryosis

B. Nabothian follicles

C. Dysplasic dyskaryosis

D. Cervical intraepithelial neoplasia

E. Cervicitis

Answer: D.Cervical intraepithelial neoplasia
103. 5 year survival for someone with stage 1a cervical carcinoma

A. 95%
B. 10%
C. 30%
D. 80%
E. 60%
Answer: A.95%
104. Cervical carcinoma spread and staging: Invasion of the lower vagina or pelvicwall, or causing ureteric obstruction
A. Stage 1a

B. Stage 4

C. Stage 3

D. Stage 2a

E. Stage 1b

Answer: C.Stage 3
105. HPV types are the most significant and account for 70% of allcervical cancers
A. 45 and 46

B. 31 and 33

C. 14 and 16

D. 16 and 18

E. 12 and 14

Answer: D.16 and 18
106. Anovulatory infertility in PCO is due to:
A. alteration of folliculogenesis caused by dysregulation of GnRH pulse generator

B. alteration of folliculogenesis caused by adrenal & ovarian hyperandrogenism
C. alteration of folliculogenesis caused by insulin resistance

D. alteration in folliculogenesis caused by alteration of ovarian growth factors

E. all of the above

Answer: E.all of the above

107. Ovarian tumors which may produce chorionic gonadotrophins include

:
A. Dysgerminoma

B. Teratoma

C. Choriocarcinoma

D. All of the above

E. None of the above

Answer: D.All of the above
108. Pathology of endometriosis may be explained by :
A. coelemic metaplasia

B. endometrial hyperplasia

C. retrograde menstruation

D. intraperitoneal immunologic deficit

E. lymphatic diffusion

Answer: C.retrograde menstruation
109. The cysts in Polycystic Ovarian syndrome are formed by:
A. Failure of atretic follicles to undergo apoptosis

B. Oocyte proliferation

C. Multiple corpus lutea

D. Cystic degeneration of ovarian cortex

E. none

Answer: A.Failure of atretic follicles to undergo apoptosis
110. An ' in situ ' stage has not been officially recognized in which of the following :
A. Ovarian carcinoma

B. Endometrial carcinoma

C. Cervical carcinoma

D. Vulvar carcinoma

E. Vaginal carcinoma

Answer: A.Ovarian carcinoma
111. The gastrointestinal primary of a Krukenberg tumour of the ovary is most oftenfound in the :
A. Gall bladder

B. Rectum

C. Pylorus

D. Colon

E. Small intestine

Answer: C.Pylorus
112. Functional ovarian cysts include:
A. Follicular cysts.

B. Endometriomas.

C. Dermoid cysts.

D. fibromas.

E. none

Answer: A.Follicular cysts.
113. In contrast to a malignant ovarian tumor, a benign tumor has which of the following gross features?
A. Excrescences on the surface.

B. Peritoneal implants.

C. Intra-cystic papillations.

D. Free mobility.

E. Capsule rupture.

Answer: D.Free mobility.
114. A 54-year-old woman is found to have endometrial hyperplasia on endometrialbiopsy. A functional ovarian tumor to be suspected is a:
A. Lipid cell tumor.

B. Granulosa-theca cell tumor.

C. Sertoli-Leydig yumor.

D. Muncious cystadenocarcinoma.

E. Polycystic ovary

Answer: B.Granulosa-theca cell tumor.
115. A uni-locular ovarian cyst measuring 4.4 cm by 4.9 cm found on routine ultrasonograrhy during the 8th week of gestation . best management for this case is
A. observation and repeated ultrasonography

B. laparoscoic aspiration of the cyst

C. immediate laparotomy and cystectomy

D. immediate laparotomy and ovariectomy

E. laparotomy and cystectomy postponed to 14 weeks

Answer: A.observation and repeated ultrasonography
116. Germ cell tumours include all the following except
A. choriocarcinoma

B. gonadoblastoma

C. endodermal sinus tumour
D. begnin cystic teratoma

E. solid teratoma

Answer: B.gonadoblastoma
117. Which is the major cause of cancer death in women?
A. Breast cancer

B. Cervical cancer

C. Endometrial cancer

D. Lung cancer

E. Ovarian cancer

Answer: A.Breast cancer
118. Endometrial carcinomas associated with estrogen therapy " caused by unopposedestrogen therapy " :
A. well differentiated

B. are deeply invasive

C. are sensitive to progesterone therapy

D. generally have poor prognosis

E. have high rates of reccurence

Answer: C.are sensitive to progesterone therapy
119. Ovarian cancer:
A. Separate FIGO staging systems exist for epithelial and sex-cord/stromal ovarian tumors

B. Granulosa Cell Tumor has an excellent prognosis because most patients present with early-stage disease

C. Meigs' syndrome consists of ascites; hydrothorax and a malignant ovarian tumor

D. Krukenberg tumours are metastatic ovarian neoplasms originating exclusively in the stomach

E. none

Answer: B.Granulosa Cell Tumor has an excellent prognosis because most patients present with early-stage disease
120. Regarding ovarian tumours
A. adenocarcinoma is more commonly bilateral than mucinous

B. the use of oral contraceptives is a risk factor for ovarian cancer

C. Sertoli-Leydig tumours of the ovary are typically estrogen secreting

D. Fat saturation MRI images are of value in diagnosing cystic teratomas

E. RI (Resistive index) values of intratumoral areas can differentiate between benign and malignant ovarian tumours

Answer: A.adenocarcinoma is more commonly bilateral than mucinous
121. A Krukenberg tumour is an ovarian neoplasm which :
A. Is primary in the ovary

B. Is associated with hydrothorax

C. Is secondary to any GIT cancer

D. Shows characteristic mucoid epithelial change

E. None of the above

Answer: D.Shows characteristic mucoid epithelial change
122. CA-125 is ?
A. A mucin-type glycoprtein

B. A ganglioside

C. A tumor-specific transplantation antigen

D. Useful for ovarian cancer screening in the general patient population

E. An antigen which is commonly expressed by mucinous ovarian carcinomas

Answer: A.A mucin-type glycoprtein
123. A young female came to you with complaint of oligomenorrhea

,hirsutism & weightgain ,US reveals bulky ovaries with subcapsular cysts.
Most likely diagnosis is
A. ovarian cancer

B. cushing syndrome

C. PCOD

D. DM

E. PID

Answer: C.PCOD
124. A large cystic tumour is detected in a woman in routine antenatal examination.The most common complication she can encounter?
A. Torsion

B. rupture

C. hemorrhage

D. infection

E. degeneration

Answer: A.Torsion
125. A 18-year-old woman comes to the physician for an annual examination. She has no complaints. She has been sexually active for the past 2 years. She uses the oral contraceptive pill for contraception. She has depression for which she takes fluoxetine. She takes no other medications and has no allergies to medications. Her family history is negative for cancer and cardiac disease. Examination is unremarkable. Which of the following screening tests should this patient most likely have?
A. Colonoscopy

B. Mammogram

C. Pap smear

D. Pelvic ultrasound

E. Sigmoidoscopy

Answer: C.Pap smear

126. Hilus or Leydig cell tumour may be associated with :
A. Reinke crystals

B. Oestrogen effect on endometrium

C. Clinical virilism

D. All of the above

E. None of the above

Answer: D.All of the above
127. A multiparous woman aged 40 years, presents with menorahagia and progressively increasing dysmenorrhoea. Most probable diagnosis is:
A. Ca Cervix

B. Ca Endometrium

C. Adenomyosis

D. DUB

E. none

Answer: C.Adenomyosis
128. Female with history of frequent micturition may be :
A. prolapse

B. incarcerated fibroma

C. pregnancy

D. a&c

E. all above .

Answer: E.all above .
129. Considering dysgerminoma all true except :
A. the commonest germ cell tumor

B. usually in young females

C. lymphatic spread is so late

D. elevate lactic dehydrogenase level .

E. none

Answer: C.lymphatic spread is so late
130. Ordering accord to the commonest cancers in female genital tract the right is :
A. cervical , endometrial ,ovarian

B. ovarian , cervical , endometrial

C. endometrial , cervical , ovarian

D. endometrial , ovarian , cervical .

E. none

Answer: C.endometrial , cervical , ovarian
131. Female came to the ER with Bp 80/60 and pulse 125 with history of acute abdomen , next step is
A. laparotomy

B. iv fluids

C. CBC

D. PV examination

E. none

Answer: B.iv fluids
132. Considering ovarian cancer :
A. surgery is preferred to be last line

B. early discovered with good prognosis

C. chemotherapy is good in most tumors

D. germ cell tumors show good response to chemotherapy

E. none

Answer: D.germ cell tumors show good response to chemotherapy
133. A 48-year-old woman has noted a small amount of irregular vaginal bleeding for the past 2

months. She has a pelvic examination that reveals no cervical lesions, and a Pap smear that shows no abnormal cells. Next, an endometrial biopsy is performed, and there is microscopic evidence for endometrial hyperplasia. An abdominal ultrasound reveals a solid right ovarian mass. Which of the following neoplasms is this woman is most likely to have?
A. Mature cystic teratoma

B. Choriocarcinoma

C. Sertoli-Leydig cell tumor

D. Fibrothecoma

E. Krukenberg tumor

Answer: D.Fibrothecoma
134. Vaginal adenocarcinomas in children is caused by
A. Virus

B. Administration of DES to pregnant mothers

C. Hormonal changes

D. All of the above

E. none

Answer: B.Administration of DES to pregnant mothers
135. Carcinoma cervix with involvement of upper 2/3 of vagina is stage
A. II

B. II B

C. III A

D. III B

E. none

Answer: A.II
136. A 47-year-old woman has noted a pressure sensation, but no pain, in her pelvic region for the past 5 months. On physical examination there is a right adnexal mass. An ultrasound scan shows a 10 cm fluid-filled cystic mass in the right ovary. A fine needle aspirate of the mass is performed and cytologic examination of clear fluid aspirated from the mass reveals clusters of malignant epithelial cells surrounding psammoma bodies. Which of the following neoplasms is she most likely to have?
A. Endometrial adenocarcinoma

B. Ovarian serous cystadenocarcinoma

C. Mesothelioma

D. Ovarian mature cystic teratoma

E. Adenocarcinoma of fallopian tube

Answer: B.Ovarian serous cystadenocarcinoma
137. Ovarian masses:

A. Are malignant in presence of ascites

B. Include benign teratomas

C. Of germ cell origin may secrete hormones

D. May be confused with develpomental abnormalities of renal tract

E. If malignant can be reliably staged pre-operatively

Answer: B.Include benign teratomas
138. A 4-year-old girl is noted to have breast enlargement and vaginal bleeding. On physical examination, she is noted to have a 9-cm pelvic mass. Which of the following is the most likely etiology?
A. Cystic teratoma

B. Dysgerminoma

C. Endodermal sinus tumor

D. Granulosa cell tumor
E. Mucinous tumor

Answer: D.Granulosa cell tumor
139. Current modes of investigation for infertility to check functioning of tubes are all of the following execpt:
A. Air insufflation

B. Sonosalpingography

C. Hysterrosalpingography

D. Laparoscopic chromotubation

E. all of the above

Answer: E.all of the above
140. Before puberty, what is the ratio between the cervical length and uterine body ?

A. 1 : 2
B. 2 : 1
C. 1 : 3
D. 1 : 4
E. none
Answer: B.2 : 1
141. As regard mastalgia:
A. in cyclic mastalgia pain is usaully max. postmenestrual

B. is treaeted surgically

C. bromocriptine may be used

D. gammaleinoliec acid is contraindicated

E. none

Answer: C.bromocriptine may be used
142. Pap smear
A. the next step in dysplastic smear is colposcopy
B. is simple but inaccurate

C. should be carried out every 5 years

D. has no role in screening of assymptomatic women

E. all of the above

Answer: A.the next step in dysplastic smear is colposcopy
143. A 40-years-old female with history of fibroid on investigation showed CIN-2 changes. Treatment of choice in this case is :
A. Hysterectomy

B. Conization

C. Cryotherapy

D. Laser ablation

E. none

Answer: A.Hysterectomy
144. Dysfunctional Uterine Bleeding (DUB) is defined as abnormal uterine bleeding ?
A. Secondary to hormonal dysfunction

B. Caused by cancer

C. In a patient with von Willebrand's disease

D. With no organic cause

E. Caused by an endometrial polyp

Answer: D.With no organic cause
145. Abnormal Uterine bleeding (AUB) is defined by all of the following except ?
A. Excessive Blood loss (>80 ml) during menses

B. Menstrual length less than 7 days

C. An interval of less than 21 days between the starts of successive menses

D. Irregular bleeding episodes between menses
E. Extended (>35 days) intervals between menses

Answer: B.Menstrual length less than 7 days
146. Dysfunctional uterine bleeding is said to present when there is bleeding due to :
A. Fibroid

B. Endometriosis

C. Irregular ripening and irregular shedding

D. Chronic endometritis

E. none

Answer: C.Irregular ripening and irregular shedding
147. Post menopausal bleeding does not occur in....
A. Use of combined OCP's

B. Atrophic vaginitis

C. Endometrial hyperplasia

D. CA-Endometrium

E. none

Answer: A.Use of combined OCP's
148. Bicornute uterus may predispose to all the following except:
A. recurrent PTL

B. primary amenorrhea

C. retention of placenta after delivery

D. menorrhagia

E. none

Answer: B.primary amenorrhea
149. A couple presented in OPD with H/0 infertility since last 2 years. Husbands semen analysis was advised. What is WHO criterion – for minimum sperm count in normal semen?
A. 10 million.

B. 20 million.

C. 30 million.

D. 40 million.

E. 70 million.

Answer: B.20 million.
150. A 23 years old primigravida presents with abdominal pain, syncope and vaginal spotting. Assessment reveals that she has an ectopic pregnancy. The most common site of pregnancy is:
A. Ampulla.

B. Isthmus.

C. Fimbrial end.

D. Abdomin.

E. Cervix.

Answer: A.Ampulla.

151. Mean age for menopause is:
A. 40 years.

B. 45 years.

C. 51 years.

D. 48 years.

E. 39 years.

Answer: C.51 years.
152. Second degree uterovaginal prolapse is characterized by:
A. Complete protrusion of uterus outside introitus.

B. Descent of genital tract within vagina.

C. Descent of genital tract upto introitus.
D. Descent of genital tract outside the introitus.

E. Descent of cervix below the ischeal spines.

Answer: D.Descent of genital tract outside the introitus.
153. A 63 years old lady presents with abdominal mass and weight loss, was diagnosed as having an ovarian tumour. The most common ovarian tumour in this woman would be:
A. Epithelial tumour.

B. Germ cell tumour.

C. Stromal tumour.

D. Sex cord tumour.

E. Trophoblastic tumour.

Answer: A.Epithelial tumour.
154. A young girl, 23 years old is presented with complaint of abdominal pain, menorrhagia and 18 weeks size mass arising from hypogastrium. The most likely diagnosis is:
A. Endometriosis.

B. Pelvic inflammatory disease.

C. Ovarian cyst.

D. Fibroid uterus.

E. Mesenteric cyst.

Answer: D.Fibroid uterus.
155. A 25 years old school teacher Para 1 wants to use oral contraceptive pills for contraception. She is asking about the mode of action of oral contraceptive pills. The mechanism of action of oral contraceptive pills is:
A. Inhibiting ovulation by suppression of serum FSH.

B. Inducing endometrial atrophy.

C. Increasing cervical mucous hostility.

D. Inducing endometritis.
E. Inhibiting prolactin.

Answer: A.Inhibiting ovulation by suppression of serum FSH.
156. Women complaining of milky whitish discharge with fishy odour. No history of itching. Most likely diagnosis is:
A. Bacterial vaginosis.

B. Trichomoniasis.

C. Candidiasis.

D. Malignancy.

E. Urinary tract infection.

Answer: A.Bacterial vaginosis.
157. A young medical student has come to you with complaints of oligomenorrrhea, hirsuitism and weight gain, ultrasound reveals bulky ovaries with sub-capsular cysts. Most likely diagnosis is:
A. Ovarian cancer.

B. Cushing's syndrome.

C. Polycystic ovarian disease.

D. Diabetes mellitus.

E. Pelvic inflammatory disease.

Answer: C.Polycystic ovarian disease.
158. A 43 year old, lecturer has come to you with complaints of heavy but regular menstrual bleeding with flooding and clots. There is no anatomical reason for heavy flow. The most effective remedy for reducing her menstrual flow is:
A. Tranexemic acid.

B. Dilatation and Curettage.

C. Depomedroxy progesterone acetate.

D. Misoprostol.

E. Ergometrine maleate.

Answer: A.Tranexemic acid.

159. A 39 years old women Para 6 has presented with complaint of post coital bleeding for the past three months. Your first investigation should be:
A. Dilatation & Curettage.

B. Cone biopsy of cervix.

C. Pap smear.

D. Colposcopy.

E. Laparoscopy.

Answer: C.Pap smear.
160. A 28 years old woman has 14 weeks size irregular uterus. She does not complain of abdominal pain or menorrhagia. Her pap smear is normal. The best next step in her management would be:
A. Continued observation.

B. Endometrial biopsy.

C. Hysterectomy.

D. Pelvic ultrasonography.

E. Laparoscopy.

Answer: D.Pelvic ultrasonography.
161. The most effective treatment of pruritis vulvae associated with atrophic vulvitis is:
A. Antihistamines.

B. Hydrocortisone.

C. Alcohol injections.

D. Tranquilizers.

E. Topical estrogen therapy.

Answer: E.Topical estrogen therapy.
162. The most common cause of rectovaginal fistula is:
A. Obstetrical.
B. Irradiation of the pelvis.

C. Carcinoma.

D. Crohn's disease.

E. Endometriosis.

Answer: A.Obstetrical.
163. A 40 years old multiparous woman complains of involuntary loss of urine associated with coughing, laughing, lifting or standing. The history is most suggestive of:
A. Fistula.

B. Stress incontinence.

C. Urge incontinence.

D. Urethral diverticulum.

E. Urinary tract infection.

Answer: B.Stress incontinence.
164. A 28 years old G3 P2 has presented with complaints of brownish vaginal discharge, passage of

vesicles and excessive vomiting. Ultrasound scan shows snowstorm appearance in uterus with no fetus. The most likely diagnosis is:
A. Septic induced abortion.

B. Twin pregnancy.

C. Gestational trophoblastic disease.

D. Ectopic pregnancy.

E. Fibroid uterus.

Answer: C.Gestational trophoblastic disease.
165. The maximum number of oogonia are formed at what ageof female life:
A. One month intrauterine.

B. Five month intrauterine.

C. At birth.

D. At puberty.

E. At 21 years of age.

Answer: B.Five month intrauterine.
166. Menarche usually occurs at age of:
A. 8 and 10 years.

B. 11 and 13 years.

C. 14 and 16 years.

D. 17 and 18 years.

E. 18 and above.

Answer: B.11 and 13 years.
167. The most common cause of vesicovaginal fistula (VVF) in under developed countries would be:
A. Obstetrical injuries.

B. Pelvic irradiation.

C. Carcinoma .

D. Haemorrhoidectomy.

E. Operative injury.

Answer: A.Obstetrical injuries.
168. A 28 year old patient complains of amenorrhea after having dilatation and curettage. The most likely diagnosis is:
A. Kallman's Syndrome.

B. Turner's Syndrome.

C. Asherman's Syndrome.

D. Pelvic inflammatory disease.

E. Anorexia nervosa.

Answer: C.Asherman's Syndrome.
169. A large cystic ovarian tumour is detected in a woman on routine antenatal check up. The most common complication she can encounter is:
A. Torsion.

B. Rupture.

C. Haemorrhage.

D. Degeneration.

E. Infection.

Answer: A.Torsion.
170. Which of the following is used to take cervical smear:
A. Colposcope.

B. Vaginoscope.

C. Ayre's spatula.

D. Laparoscope.

E. Forceps.

Answer: C.Ayre's spatula.
171. Normal duration of menstrual cycle is:
A. 1-3 days.

B. 1-4 days.

C. 2-7 days.

D. 7-10 days.

E. 1-2 days.

Answer: C.2-7 days.
172. a 20 year old medical student presents with five years history of weight gain, irregular periods and worsening fascial hair. What is the most likely diagnosis?
A. Polycystic ovarian disease.

B. Hypothyroidism.

C. Obesity.

D. Cushing's Syndrome.

E. Nephrotic Syndrome.

Answer: A.Polycystic ovarian disease.
173. 28 years old woman with previous history of having baby with Down's Syndrome is now 12 weeks pregnant. Which of the following would you suggest to her:
A. Amniocentesis.

B. Obstetric ultrasound.

C. Chorionic villus sampling.

D. Fetal blood sampling.

E. Wait till eighteen weeks for detailed ultrasound and amniocentesis.

Answer: C.Chorionic villus sampling.
174. A newly married girl comes to gynae OPD with history of dysuria, burning, micturition and sore perineum. What is your likely diagnosis:
A. Trichomonas vaginalis.

B. Candida infection.

C. Trauma due to coitus.

D. Honey moon cystitis.

E. Genital herpes.

Answer: D.Honey moon cystitis.
175. Gonadotropin releasing hormone (GnRH) stimulates the release of:
A. ACTH.

B. Growth hormone.

C. Leutinising Hormone (LH).
D. Thyroid stimulating hormone (TSH).

E. Opiate peptides.

Answer: C.Leutinising Hormone (LH).
176. Serum prolactin levels are highest in which of the following conditions:
A. Menopause.

B. Ovulation.

C. Parturition.

D. Sleep.

E. Running.

Answer: C.Parturition.
177. Main uterine support is:
A. Uterosacral ligaments.

B. Round ligaments.

C. Transverse cervical ligaments.

D. Ovarian ligaments.

E. Broad ligaments.

Answer: C.Transverse cervical ligaments.
178. The most likely cause of abnormal uterine bleeding in 13years old girl is:
A. Uterine cancer.

B. Ectopic pregnancy.

C. Anovulation.

D. Systemic bleeding diatheses.

E. Trauma.

Answer: C.Anovulation.
179. Which of the following pubertal event would occur even in the absence of ovarian estrogen production:

A. Thelarche.

B. Menarche.

C. Pubarche.

D. Skeletal growth.

E. Vaginal cornification.

Answer: C.Pubarche.
180. 58 years old woman has presented with complaints of postmenopausal bleeding for the past two weeks. The most essential investigation would be:
A. Colposcopy.

B. Pap smear.

C. Cone biopsy.

D. D & C (dilatation & Curettage).

E. Hysteroscopy.

Answer: D.D & C (dilatation & Curettage).
181. The most common symptom of endometrial hyperplasia is:
A. Vaginal discharge.

B. Vaginal bleeding.

C. Amenorrhea.

D. Pelvic pain.

E. Abdominal distention.

Answer: B.Vaginal bleeding.
182. 56 years old woman has come to you with the complaints of hot flushes irritability, joint pains with lack of sleep. Most appropriate treatment would be:
A. Hysterectomy.

B. Vitamins.

C. Combined oestrogen, progesterone preparations.

D. Phytooestrogens.

E. Selective estrogen receptor modulators (SERMS).

Answer: C.Combined oestrogen, progesterone preparations.
183. Which of the following is used as an emergency contraceptive:
A. Combined oral contraceptive pills.

B. Progesterone only.

C. Depoprovera.

D. Levonorgestril (EM-Kit).

E. Ergometrine.

Answer: D.Levonorgestril (EM-Kit).

PART-II

1. Lady with infertility with bilateral tubal block at cornua. Best method of management is :

a. Laparoscopy & Hysteroscopy
b. Hydrotubation
c. IVF
d. Tuboplasty

Answer : A; Laparoscopy is done for proper assessment & to exclude active infection or TB.

2. Women with postmenopausal bleeding need endometrial sampling if endometrial on US is thicker than

a. 1mm
b. 2mm
c. 5mm
d. 8mm
e. 10mm

Answer : C ; endometrial thickness in menopause > 5 mm is suspicious for hyperplasia

3. Which of the following change in puberty is influenced by the estrogen:

a. Growth of the acinar buds of the breast
b. Epiphyseal fusion
c. Proliferatve phase
d. All of the above
e. None of the above

Answer : D : Estrogen is critical for epiphyseal fusion in both young men and women . Proliferative phase also continues under the effect of ovarian estrogen produced by the maturating follicles till ovulation occurs . Estrogen also can affects both ductal and glandular " acinar " system of breast .

4. Sub urethral diverticula may occur as a sequelae to infection of:

a. Bartholin's gland
b. Skene's gland
c. Clitoral gland
d. Vulvovaginal gland

Answer : B ; Periurethral glands (Skene's glands) are tubuloalveolar structures along the dorsolateral aspect that drain into the distal two thirds of the urethra. Repeated infection and obstruction of these glands lead to formation of suburethral cysts or abscesses that can rupture into the urethral lumen.

5. Glycogen is seen in the lumina of endometrial glands :

a. During the luteal phase
b. During pregnancy only
c. During pre and post ovulatory
d. During proliferative phase only
e. At the time of ovulation only

Answer : A ; During the follicular, or proliferative phase, endometrial glands are elongated with narrow lumens and their epithelial cells contain some glycogen. Glycogen, however, is not secreted during the follicular phase.
At the beginning of the luteal phase, progesterone induces the endometrial glands to secrete glycogen, mucus, and other substances.

6. The Wolfian duct in the female :

a. Develops into the fallopian tube
b. Forms the ovary
c. Forms the round ligament
d. Regresses and becomes vestigial
e. None of the above

Answer : D ; due to the absence of testosterone in females , the Wollfian duct will regress and is represented in the female adult by the Gartner`s duct

7. Large amount of alkaline phosphatase may be demonstrated in the endometrium of :

a. Decidua
b. Secretory phase
c. Proliferative phase
d. All of the above
e. None of the above

Answer: C : Alkaline phosphatase activity is markedly stimulated by estrogen which is responsible for the proliferative phase.

8. Oxytocin and vasopressin are transferred from hypothalamus to neurohypophysis through:

a. Venous channels
b. Lymphatics
c. Nerve axons
d. All of the above
e. None of the above Answer : C

9. The levator ani muscle :

a. Is a voluntary muscle
b. Is attached laterally to the "white line of the pelvis "
c. Is composed of pubococcygeus and iliococcygeus muscle
d. Contracts to prevent spillage of urine during strain
e. All of the above Answer : E

10. The function of round ligament is :

a. Vestigial with no apparent function
b. To prevent retrodisplacement of the uterus
c. To prevent uterine prolapse
d. To provide nerve supply of the upper vagina
e. None of the above

Answer : B ; The function of the round ligament is the maintenance of the anteversion of the uterus during pregnancy.

11. The definitive epithelium of vagina is derived from :

a. Wolfian duct
b. Mullerian duct
c. Urogenital epithelium
d. Coelomic epithelium Answer : C

12. Causes of post partum amenorrhoea may be :

a. Anorexia nervosa
b. Cervical atresia
c. Chlorpromazaine therapy
d. Any of the above
e. None of the above

Answer : D : Chlorpromazine has antidopaminergic effect >> hyperprolactinemea >> anovulation >> ammenorrhea
N.B. Cervical atresia is an extremely rare condition in which the cervical canal is missing at birth.

13. The cyclic production of pituitary hormones is dependant upon:

a. Normal menstruation
b. An intact pituitary- portal system
c. An adult anterior pituitary gland

d. All of the above
e. None of the above

Answer: B

14. The clots passed with menorrhagia perhaps indicate
a. No endometrial regeneration
b. No terminal arteriolar spasm
c. Large amount of bleeding
d. All of the above
e. None of the above Answer : C

15. Monilial vagintis occurs frquently during pregnancy because :
a. Glycosuria is commoner
b. The vagina contains more glycogen
c. Higher vaginal acidity suppresses other organisms
d. All of the above
e. None of the above

Answer : D : Candida flourishes in acidic media as during pregnancy and long term use of OCPs due to increased glycogen content of vaginal epithelium , allowing for more production of lactic acid by lactobacilli

16. Physical exam reveals the uterus to be about 6 wk size. Vaginal bleeding is scanty with no discernible tissue in the cervical os. There are no palpable adnexal masses. The uterus is mildly tender. Ultrasonographic exam does not reveal a gestational sac. Which of the following should be recommended?
a. Dilatation & curettage.
b. Culdocentesis.
c. Observation followed by serial B-HCG determinations.
d. Diagnostic laparoscopy.
e. Laparotomy Answer : D

17. Which of the following statements is incorrect regarding levonorgestrel releasing intrauterine system:
a. There is increased incidence of menorrhagia
b. This system can be used as hormone replacement therapy
c. This method is useful for the treatment of endometerial hyperplasia
d. Irregular uterine bleeding can be problem initially

Answer : A : Levonorgestrel is a progestin , Named levonorgestrel because it is the levorotatory form of norgestrel. It can be used as hormone replacement therapy and for treatment of endometerial hyperplasia as it induces endometrial atrophic changes , so it's less likely to cause menorrhagia.

18. Myxoma peritonei may occur as a consequence of rupture of which ovarian cyst ?
a. Dermoid
b. Struma ovarii
c. Serous cystadenoma
d. Mucinous cystadenoma
e. Cystadenofibroma Answer : D

19. Lutein and theca lutein cysts may be associated with all the following except :
a. Mole
b. Chorionepithelioma
c. Stein-leventhal syndrome(PCO)
d. Pregnancy
e. Abortion Answer : C

20. The site of primary infection in patients with pelvic tuberculosis is usually

a. Tubal
b. Uterine
c. Cervical
d. Ovarian
e. Lungs Answer : E

21. The preferred treatment of ruptured tubo-ovarian abscess is :
a. Cul-de-sac drainage
b. Removal of uterus , tubes and involved ovary
c. Removal of uterus , tubes and ovaries
d. Removal of ruptured tube and ovary
e. Removal of adenexae and drainage Answer:C

N.B: the ttt of ruptured tubo-ovarian abcess depends on age,if young we remove the affected tube & ovary,if old we remove the uterus & both tubes & ovaries.
22. The cysts of Stein -Leventhal ovary or PCOD are of which kind?
a. Lutein
b. Germinal inclusion
c. Follicular
d. Theca lutein

e. Endometrial Answer : C

23. Clinical findings of PCOD include all except :
a. Obesity
b. Olgomenorrhoea
c. Infertility
d. Tall stature Answer : D

24. Pyogenic infections of genital tract usually spread via :
a. Mucous membrane
b. Veins
c. Lymphatics
d. Fistulous tracts
e. B+C Answer : E

25. Presence of pyometra in a post menopausal females strongly suggests:
a. Diabetes mellitus
b. Degenerating myoma
c. Senile endometritis
d. Malignancy
e. Sexual promiscuity

Answer : D : A pyometra is a collection of pus distending the uterine cavity. It occurs principally when there is a stenosed cervical os, usually due to uterine or cervical malignancy, & pus formed of infected necrotic malignant tissue.
26. The most common symptom associated with adenomyosis is :
a. Infertility
b. Menorrhagia
c. Haematometra
d. Dyspareunia
e. Metrorrhagia

Answer : B : Due to increased uterine size and endometrial surface area
27. Adenomyosis is often associated with all of the following except :

a. Endometrial hyperplasia
b. Myoma
c. Endometriosis
d. Mymetrial hypertrophy

e. Subinvolution of uterus Answer : E

28. Interstitial uterine myomas most often cause menorrhagia due to :
a. Secondary degeneration
b. Rupture into endometrial cavity
c. Pressure necrosis
d. Inhibition of uterine contractility
e. Prolapse

Answer : D : Due to the mechanical interference with uterine contractility
29. There is a 5% incidence of primary extrauterine malignancy associated with endometrial cancer, the most frequent site for such is :
a. Stomach
b. lung
c. Breast
d. Bone
e. Spleen Answer : C

30. The cause of virilizing adrenal hyperplasia is :
a. Defect in cortisol synthesis
b. defect in ACTH synthesis
c. Defect in testosterone synthesis
d. All of the above
e. None of the above Answer : A

31. Anterior pituitary function may be blocked by:
a. Blood levels of steroids
b. Emotional factors
c. Sensory stimuli
d. All of the above
e. None of the above Answer : D

32. Subnuclear vaculoes in the endometrial mucosa are evidence of activity of:
a. Cholesterol
b. Progesterone
c. Pregnendiol
d. Androstenendione

e. Oestrogen

Answer : B : In the early secretory phase " under the effect of progesterone " ; vacuoles containing subnuclear intracytoplasmic granules appear in glandular cells .
33. Common ovulation induced drugs are
a. Clomiphene citrate
b. Tamoxifen or the newer letrozole
c. Gonadotrophins
d. GnRh analogue down regulation protocols
e. All of the above Answer : E

34. The commonest cause of death in cancer cervix is :
a. Infection
b. Uraemia
c. Haemorrhage
d. Cachexia
e. Distant metastasis Answer : B

35. Failure to find sperm in postcoital examination may be due to :
a. Excessive oestrogen effect on cervical mucous
b. Excessive vaginal lactic acid
c. Oligospermia
d. All of the above
e. None of the above Answer : C

36. The differential diagnosis of vaginal cysts include :
a. Cystocele
b. Urethral diverticulum
c. Urethrocoele
d. All of the above
e. None of the above Answer : D

37. Factors in cervical cancer development EXCEPT:
a. HIV infection
b. Chlamydia infection
c. Breast cancer
d. Smoking

e. Immunosuppression Answer : C

38. A synthetic progestin. What is the most likely explanation for the contraceptive action of this drug?
a. Replacement of the LH surge by an FSH surge.
b. Abolition of the LH surge
c. Enhanced positive feedback of the hypothalamic-pituitary-gonadal axis.
d. Increased conversion of testosterone to estradiol.
e. Inadequate decidualization of the uterus.

Ansewer : E: N.B:inadequate decidualization=pseudodecidualization
39. All of the following mechanisms might account for a reduced risk of upper genital tract infection in users of progestin releasing IUDs, except:
a. Reduced retrograde menstruation
b. Decreased ovulation
c. Thickened cervical mucus
d. Decidual changes in the endometrium
e. All of the above Answer :E

40. Non-neoplastic ovarian cysts include all of the following except:
a. follicular cyst
b. theca lutein cyst
c. dermoid cyst
d. corpus luteum cyst
e. endmetroid cyst Answer : C

41. Which of the following ovarian tumor is most prone to undergo torsion during pregnancy?

a. Serous cystadenoma
b. Mucinous cystadenoma
c. Dermoid cyst
d. Theca lutein cyst

Answer : C : As most dermoid cysts have a long pedicle that makes them more liable to complications as torsion .

42. Magnesium sulphate toxicity include all EXCEPT:

a. CNS depression
b. This drug acts only on motor end plate

c. Respiratory depression
d. muscle relaxant

Answer : B : MgSo4 acts by inhibition of neuromuscular transmission and CNS depression

43. In DUB all are right except,:

a. may be associated with hypothyroidism
b. may be associated with post-menopausal bleeding
c. may be associated with functional ovarian cysts
d. may present as menorrhagia
e. may be present as metropathia hemorrhagica Answer : B

44. Metabolic causes of anovulatory DUB include all except :

a. Hypothyroidism
b. Halban's syndrome
c. Cushing's syndrome
d. Hyperthyroidism
e. diabetes mellitus Answer : B

45. The primary drainage of the lower vagina is to :

a. external iliac nodes
b. Sacral nodes
c. Femoral nodes
d. superficial inguinal nodes
e. internal iliac nodes

Answer: D : The upper 1/3 follows lymphatic drainage of the cervix , the lower 1/3 drains to the inguinal LNs & the middle 1/3 drains in both upper and lower directions .

46. The most common causative organism in acute bartholinitis is

a. Staphylococcus
b. Streptococcus
c. Colon bacillus
d. Gonococcus
e. Trichomonas Answer :D

47. The uterine artery supplies the

a. Vagina
b. Lower cevix
c. Ovary

d. All of the above
e. None of the above

Answer : D : The uterine artery supplies round ligament of the uterus , ovary "Ovarian branches" , uterus "arcuate vessels", vaginaVaginal branches- azygos arteries of the vagina" and uterine tube "Tubal branch"

48. Common accompaniments salpingitis are :

a. Pelvic mass
b. Bleeding
c. Pain
d. All of the above
e. None of the above Answer: C:is the most right

a:pelvic mass if tubo-ovarian abscess has developed b:bleeding is not common

49. he ovary of new born may contain :

a. Small folicular cysts
b. Corpora lutea
c. Lutenized grnulosa cells
d. All of the above
e. None of the above

Answer : E : contains primordial follicles

50. Cervical amputation :

a. Is followed frequently by abortion
b. Is associated with high incidence of post operative sterility
c. Is not frequently followed by cervical dystocia in patients who become pregnant
d. All of the above
e. None of the above Answer D

51. The effect of ovarian steroid on anterior pituitary is

a. Direct stimulation
b. Direct inhibition
c. Mediated via hypothalamus
d. Unknown
e. Direct stimulation and inhibition Answer:C

52. What are the signs of ovulation on Ultrasonography :

a. Irregular follicle wall
b. Collapse of follicle
c. Fluid in cul de sac
d. All of the above
e. None of the above Answer:D

53. The uterus is held in anteflexed position by :

a. The ventral pull of round ligament
b. The dorsal pull of uterosacral ligaments
c. Its weight
d. All of the above
e. None of the above Answer:D

54. The most common symptom of adenomyosis is :

a. Dysmenorrhoea
b. Menorrhagia
c. Pain
d. Fever
e. None of the above Answer:B

55. The commonest cause of stress incontinence is

a. Constipation
b. Raised intra abdominal pressure
c. Congenital weakness of sphincter
d. Childbirth trauma
e. Estrogen deficiency

Answer: D : Most cases of stress incontinence are due to weakened pelvic floor muscles. The common reason for the pelvic floor muscles to become weakened is childbirth.

56. Perforation of the uterus while doing endometrial biopsy in non pregnant uterus, needs

a. Laparoscopy
b. Observation
c. Immediate laparotomy
d. Hysterectomy Answer :A

57. Least common type of uterine anomaly in patients with recurrent pregnancy loss :

a. Unicornuate
b. Arcuate
c. Septate
d. Bicornuate
e. Didelphys Answer:A :

unicornuate uterus is the least commen uterine anomaly in which pregnancy could occur.

58. Diagnosis of stress incontinence coded
by which of the following before taking the patient for surgery
a. History
b. Subjective demonstration of stress incontinence
c. Objective demonstration of stress incontinence
d. Urodynamic studies Answer:D

59. The following are the factors associated with CIN EXCEPT

a. Onset of coitus at early stage
b. Multiple sexual partners
c. Lower socioeconomic status
d. Nulliparity
e. H/o veneral disease

Answer:D : Multiparity is believed to be a risk factor for cervical cancer (CC).
Women who have had 3 or more full-term pregnancies have an increased risk of developing cervical cancer. One theory is that these women had to have had unprotected intercourse to get pregnant, so they may have had more exposure to HPV. Also, studies have pointed to hormonal changes during pregnancy as possibly making women more susceptible to HPV infection or cancer growth. Another thought is that the immune system of pregnant women might be weaker, allowing for HPV infection and cancer growth.
also multiple pregnancies >> multiple vaginal deliveries >> multiple cervical traumatas

60. Best treatment for severe stress incontinence without prolapse is

a. Pelvic floor exercise
b. Kelly's repair
c. Burch colposuspension
d. MMK operation
e. Urethral collagen implant Answer:B

61. Bartholin's gland duct opens in.....

a. Upper third of labia majora

b. Middle third of labia majora
c. Upper third of labia minora
d. Middle third of labia minora Answer:D

62.A 19-year-old female comes to the physician because of left lower quadrant pain for 2 months. She states that she first noticed the pain 2 months ago but now it seems to be growing worse. She has had no changes in bowel or bladder function. She has no fevers or chills and no nausea, vomiting, or diarrhea. The pain is intermittent and sometimes feels like a dull pressure. Pelvic examination is significant for a left adnexal mass that is mildly tender. Urine hCG is negative. Pelvic ultrasound shows a 6 cm complex left adnexal mass with features consistent with a benign cystic teratoma (dermoid). Which of the following is the most appropriate next step in management?
a. Repeat pelvic examination in 1 year
b. Repeat pelvic ultrasound in 6 weeks
c. Prescribe the oral contraceptive pill
d. Perform hysteroscopy
e. perform laparotomy Answer:E

63.A 54-year-old woman comes to the physician for an annual examination. She has no complaints. For the past year, she has been taking tamoxifen for the prevention of breast cancer. She was started on this drug after her physician determined her to be at high risk on the basis of her strong family history, nulliparity, and early age at menarche. She takes no other medications. Examination is within normal limits. Which of the following is this patient most likely to develop while taking tamoxifen?
a. Breast cancer
b. Elevated LDL cholesterol
c. Endometrial changes
d. Myocardial infarction
e. Osteoporosis

Answer:C : Tamoxifen is an antagonist of the estrogen receptor in breast tissue via its active metabolite, hydroxytamoxifen. In other tissues such as the endometrium, it behaves as an agonist, and thus may be characterized as a mixed agonist/antagonist.So , even though it is an antagonist in breast tissue it acts as partial agonist on the endometrium and has been linked to endometrial cancer in some women .

64.A 62-year-old woman comes to the physician because of bleeding from the vagina. She states that her last menstrual period came 11 years ago and that she has had no bleeding since that time. She has hypertension and type 2 diabetes mellitus.
Examination shows a mildly obese woman in no apparent distress. Pelvic examination is unremarkable. An endometrial biopsy is performed that shows grade I endometrial adenocarcinoma. Which of the following is the most appropriate next step in management?
a. Chemotherapy
b. Cone biopsy
c. Dilation and curettage
d. Hysteroscopy
e. Hysterectomy Answer:E

65. Ovarian precursors of oestradiol include :
a. Oestrone
b. Androstenedione
c. Testosterone
d. All of the above
e. None of the above Answer:D

66. Female patient with endometrial hyperplasia could be all of these except:
a. thecoma
b. fibroma
c. Brenner tumor
d. follicular cyst .

Answer:B : Follicular cyst and thecoma are functioning secreting estrogen . Also , Occasionally some of Brenner tumors may secrete estrogen .
67. Endometroid cyst, on examination:
a. adenexal tenderness
b. cyst felt in thin people
c. cyst fixed and tender
d. all of the above . Answer:D

68. Considering epithelial neoplasm of the ovaries all true except :
a. the commonest
b. mucinous cystadenoma lined by tubal epithelium
c. Brenner tumor lined by urinary tract epithelium
d. embryologically arise from wolffian epithelium .

Answer: B : mucinous cystadenoma lined by tall columnar mucous secreting epithelium (as cervix)
69. The Commonest ovarian neoplasm complicated with torsion during pregnancy:
a. fibroma
b. teratoma
c. simple serous cyst
d. thecoma .

Answer:B: As most teratomas have long pedicles make them more liable to complications especially torsion .
70. Female patient with acute abdomen , CBC normal , B-HCG negative , No vaginal bleeding , Mostly is :
a. hemorrhagic teratoma
b. disturbed ectopic pregnancy
c. appendicitis
d. peritonitis . Answer:A

71. Considering mucinous cystadenoma :
a. the commonest neoplasm
b. usually bilateral
c. sometimes fill the entire abdominal cavity
d. lined by tubal epithelium .

Answer:C : mucinous cystadenoma are known to reach huge sizes some times filling the entire abdominal cavity
72. Considering Brenner tumor all true except :
a. potential malignant is common
b. histologically has epithelial nests and coffe bean nuclei
c. vaginal bleeding reported with it
d. usually in childbearing women

Answer:D : Brenner tumors are more prevalent > 40 years .
73. Considering Meig's syndrome it is associated with :
a. ovarian fibroma
b. left side pleural effusion
c. ascitis

d. a&b
e. a&c

Answer:E : Meig`s syndrome is the association of ovarian fibroma , right sided pleural effusion and ascites.

74. Considering malignant ovarian neoplasm histologically may be all except :
a. epithelial tumors
b. germ cells tumor
c. cystic and solid tumors
d. sex cord tumors .

Answer:C: consistency of the tumour appears grossly & not microscopically .

75. For endometrial cyst all true except :
a. choclate cyst on TVS
b. laparoscope is indicated
c. C125 is a specific test
d. associated with dysmenoorrhoea . Answer:C

76. Female patient with history of induction of ovulation present with tender lower abdominal pain and discomfort , TVS show cyst , Next step is :
a. assurance sending home
b. hold ovarian stimulatin drug
c. laparotomy
d. non of the above . Answer:B

77. Considering endometroid cyst :
a. not uncommon
b. due to menstrual reaction
c. torsion is common
d. a&b .
e. all the above Answer:D

tortion is uncommon as this cyst is fixed by surrounding adhesions.

78. Considering endometrial cyst ttt all true except :
a. GNRH is of benefit
b. laparosope idicated in small cyst
c. laparotomy is preferred
d. recurrence is not common Answer:D

79. Considering the follicular cyst it is rarely associated with :
a. endometrial hyperplasia

b. acute abdomen
c. polycystic ovary
d. On PV in obese patient it may rupture . Answer:B

80. Female patient with history of endometriosis , menstrual disorders complaining from pain on right iliac fossa , on examination there was tenderness on right iliac fossa with no rebound pain no rigidity , on CBC it was normal , most likely :
a. peritonitis
b. appendicitis
c. follicular cyst
d. non of the above Answer:C

81. Considering a case of follicular cyst it need all of following except :

a. assurance follow up
b. OCP
c. usually surgical removal
d. repeated US Answer:C

82. Considering the follicular cyst all of following is true except :
a. associated with metropathia hemorrhagica
b. OCP indicated in ttt
c. the second common functional cyst
d. TAS is the gold standard diagnostic method Answer:C : It's the most common

83. Considering the endometroid cyst :
a. associated with dysmenorrhoea
b. associated with pelvic pain
c. associatd with pelvic endometriosis
d. All of the above Answer:D

84. Female patient with history of hydatiform and complaining of lower abdominal pain , on examination there was tenderness on palpation and the lab result show high level of HCG , most likely to be :
a. follicular cyst
b. theca lutein cyst
c. corpus luteum cyst

d. non of the above . Answer:B

85. A 29-year-old G4P4 is found to have an abnormal smear signed out as atypical glandular cells, favouring neoplasia. She undergoes a colposcopy with cervical biopsies. One of the ectocervical biopsies demonstrated adenocarcinima in the situ. The most appropriate next step is:
a. Vaginal hysterectomy
b. Radical hysterectomy/Radiotherapy
c. Cold-knife conization of the cervix
d. Loop excision of the cervical tranformation zone Answer: C

86. The following about human papilloma virus (HPV) infection are correct EXCEPT:
a. It is the most common viral STDs.
b. It may lead CIN and cervical cancer.
c. It is due to RNA virus.
d. Infection may be warty or flat condyloma.
e. Infection is usually associated with others STDs. Answer:C : HPV is a DNA virus.

87. The lymphatic drainage of the cervix is to the following lymph nodes EXCEPT:
a. The femoral lymph nodes.
b. The internal iliac lymph nodes.
c. The para-cervical lymph nodes.
d. The pre-sacral lymh nodes.
e. The Obturator lymph nodes Answer:A

88. The commonest secondary change in uterine fibroids is:
a. Fatty degeneration
b. Myxomatous degeneration.
c. Hyaline degeneration
d. Cystic degeneration
e. Calcification

Answer:C : Hyaline degeneration is commonly occur in the centre due to poor vascularity .
89. The following is correct about the ovarian ligaments:
a. Contain ureters.
b. Contain ovarian arteries.
c. Are attached laterally to pelvic wall.

d. Lie anterior to the broad ligament.
e. Are homologous to part of the gubernaculums testis in the male Answer:B

90. The severity of CIN is graded
a. 1-3
b. 1a-4a
c. I-III+ I-IV
d. A-C Answer:A

91. Cervical polyps
a. causes spontaneous abortion
b. are cause of antepartum hge
c. cause watery vaginal discharge
d. are covered by squamous epithelium
e. cause intermenstrual bleeding

Answer:E : Cervical polyps often show no symptoms. Where there are symptoms, they include intermenstrual bleeding(metrorrhagia), abnormally heavy menstrual bleeding (menorrhagia), vaginal bleeding in post-menopausal women, bleeding after sexual intercourse and thick white vaginal or yellowish discharge
92. Involves pelvic LN clearance, hysterectomy, removal of the parametrium and the upper third of the vagina.
a. Wartman's hysterectomy
b. Wertheim's hysterectomy
c. Wertheims Trachelectomy
d. Radical trachelectomy
e. Trachelems hysterectomy Answer:B

93. 5 year survival for someone with stage 3-4 cervical carcinoma
a. 10-30%!!!
b. 80-95%
c. 2-10%
d. 65-80%
e. 45-60%
Answer:A
94. Cervical carcinoma spread and staging: Microinvasion of the basement membrane,

<7mm across, with no lymph/vascular space invasion

a. Stage 1b
b. Stage 3
c. Stage 4
d. Stage 1a
e. Stage 2a Answer:D

95. Acetic acid turns a portion of the cervix _ in a patient with a CIN
a. Green
b. Blue

c. Brown
d. Orange
e. White Answer:E

96. Typical cells are found only in the lower third of the epithelium
a. CIN III
b. CIN I
c. CIN V
d. CIN IV
e. CIN II Answer:E

typical cells are only found in lower third of epithelium. therefore atypical cells occupy the upper 2/3
97. A 42-year-old G4P4 has had postcoital bleeding for the past four months. She has not had a Pap test since the delivery of her last child 7 years ago. Speculum examination shows a vaginal discharge and a 1 cm exophytic lesion of the posterior cervical lip. The most appropriate next step is:
a. Perform a Pap smear
b. Perform a cold-knife conization
c. Give the patient a course of intravaginal Metronidazole gel followed by re- examination in 6 weeks
d. Perform a punch biopsy of the lesion Answer:D

98. The area where cervical carcinoma usually originates
a. Neoplastic zone
b. Metaplastic field
c. Retrograde area
d. Transformation zone

e. Transition field Answer:D

99. Cervical carcinoma is most common between the ages of
a. 45-55
b. 16-18
c. 18-22
d. 35-45
e. 25-35
Answer:A
100. Cervical carcinoma characteristically spreads in the
a. Tissue
b. Lymph
c. Bone
d. Blood
e. Mucus

Answer:B : Lymphatic spread by both permeation and embolization .
101. Which of the following is thought to be protective against CIN?
a. HIV
b. Oral contraceptive usage
c. Long term sexual abstinence
d. Smoking
e. Long term steroid use Answer:C

102. Cervical carcinoma that can be treated with cone biopsy
a. Stage 5
b. Stage 1a
c. Stage 3

d. Stage 2a
e. Stage 4a Answer:B

103. The presence of atypical cells within the squamous epithelium
a. Cervical dyskaryosis
b. Nabothian follicles
c. Dysplasic dyskaryosis
d. Cervical intraepithelial neoplasia
e. Cervicitis
Answer d

104. 5 year survival for someone with stage 1a cervical carcinoma
a. 95%
b. 10%
c. 30%
d. 80%
e. 60%
Answer:A

105. Cervical carcinoma spread and staging: Invasion of the lower vagina or pelvic wall, or causing ureteric obstruction
a. Stage 1a
b. Stage 4
c. Stage 3
d. Stage 2a
e. Stage 1b

Answer:C

106. HPV types_ are the most significant and account for 70% of all cervical cancers
a. 45 and 46
b. 31 and 33
c. 14 and 16
d. 16 and 18
e. 12 and 14

Answer:D

107. Anovulatory infertility in PCO is due to:
a. alteration of folliculogenesis caused by dysregulation of GnRH pulse generator
b. alteration of folliculogenesis caused by adrenal & ovarian hyperandrogenism
c. alteration of folliculogenesis caused by insulin resistance
d. alteration in folliculogenesis caused by alteration of ovarian growth factors
e. alteration of folliculogenesis caused by hyper-estrogenism f.all of the above

Answer:F: Alteration of folliculogenesis means no ovulation will occur and in pco it is called anovulatory PCO
The PCO syndrome is due to several initiating theories and theories of pathogenesis not necessary present all of them in all patients but which is constant is hyperandrogenism particularly testosterone all predisposing factors as mentioned from B to E Produces the same increase in androgen.

about the A dysregulation means disturbance in the function of the release of GnRH pulse either

spontaneous or due to negative feed back from peripheral hormones as cases are associated with increase LH levels
So combination of one or more of these factors leads to pco

108. Ovarian tumors which may produce chorionic gonadotrophins include :
a. Dysgerminoma
b. Teratoma
c. Choriocarcinoma
d. All of the above
e. None of the above

Answer:D

109. Pathology of endometriosis may be explained by :
a. coelemic metaplasia
b. endometrial hyperplasia
c. retrograde menstruation
d. intraperitoneal immunologic deficit
e. lymphatic diffusion
Answer:C:retrograde menstruation is the most acceptable theory.

110. The cysts in Polycystic Ovarian syndrome are formed by:
a. Failure of atretic follicles to undergo apoptosis
b. Oocyte proliferation
c. Multiple corpus lutea
d. Cystic degeneration of ovarian cortex

Answer:A

111. An ' in situ ' stage has not been officially recognized in which of the following :
a. Ovarian carcinoma
b. Endometrial carcinoma
c. Cervical carcinoma
d. Vulvar carcinoma
e. Vaginal carcinoma

Answer:A

112. The gastrointestinal primary of a Krukenberg tumour of the ovary is most often found in the :
a. Gall bladder
b. Rectum
c. Pylorus

d. Colon
e. Small intestine

Answer:C : The primary is usually in the pylorus of the stomach , less commonly in the colon , breast or biliary tract .

113. Functional ovarian cysts include:
a. Follicular cysts.
b. Endometriomas.
c. Dermoid cysts.
d. fibromas.
Answer: A : Follicular cysts lined by granulose cells that may continue to produce estrogen .

114. In contrast to a malignant ovarian tumor, a benign tumor has which of the following gross features?
a. Excrescences on the surface.
b. Peritoneal implants.
c. Intra-cystic papillations.
d. Free mobility.
e. Capsule rupture.

Answer:D

115. A 54-year-old woman is found to have endometrial hyperplasia on endometrial biopsy. A functional ovarian tumor to be suspected is a:
a. Lipid cell tumor.
b. Granulosa-theca cell tumor.
c. Sertoli-Leydig yumor.
d. Muncious cystadenocarcinoma.
e. Polycystic ovary

Answer:B

116. A uni-locular ovarian cyst measuring 4.4 cm by 4.9 cm found on routine ultrasonograrhy during the 8th week of gestation . best management for this case is
a. observation and repeated ultrasonography
b. laparoscoic aspiration of the cyst
c. immediate laparotomy and cystectomy
d. immediate laparotomy and ovariectomy
e. laparotomy and cystectomy postponed to 14 weeks

Answer:A

117. Germ cell tumours include all the following except

a. choriocarcinoma
b. gonadoblastoma
c. endodermal sinus tumour
d. begnin cystic teratoma
e. solid teratoma

Answer:B

118. Which is the major cause of cancer death in women?
a. Breast cancer
b. Cervical cancer
c. Endometrial cancer
d. Lung cancer
e. Ovarian cancer

Answer:A

119. Endometrial carcinomas associated with estrogen therapy " caused by unopposed estrogen therapy " :
a. well differentiated
b. are deeply invasive
c. are sensitive to progesterone therapy
d. generally have poor prognosis
e. have high rates of reccurence

Answer:C

120. Ovarian cancer:
a. Separate FIGO staging systems exist for epithelial and sex-cord/stromal ovarian tumors
b. Granulosa Cell Tumor has an excellent prognosis because most patients present with early-stage disease
c. Meigs' syndrome consists of ascites; hydrothorax and a malignant ovarian tumor
d. Krukenberg tumours are metastatic ovarian neoplasms originating exclusively in the stomach
Answer:B :
1) The same FIGO staging system is used not a separate one
2) as granulosa cell tumour is slowly growing
3) a benign not malignant tumour
4) not exclusevely in the stomach

121. Pelvic ultrasound is helpful in the diagnosis of:
a. Endometrial carcinoma
b. Asherman's syndrome

c. Ascites
d. Ovulation detection
e. Endometriosis

Answer:D

122. Regarding ovarian tumours
a. adenocarcinoma is more commonly bilateral than mucinous
b. the use of oral contraceptives is a risk factor for ovarian cancer
c. Sertoli-Leydig tumours of the ovary are typically estrogen secreting
d. Fat saturation MRI images are of value in diagnosing cystic teratomas
e. RI (Resistive index) values of intratumoral areas can differentiate between benign and malignant ovarian tumours

Answer : Most correct answer is A B wrong. The reverse is right
C wrong. Mostly testosterone
D wrong fat suppression MRI not saturation
E wrong as although ri can differentiate but not all cases as it is misleading

123. A Krukenberg tumour is an ovarian neoplasm which :
a. Is primary in the ovary
b. Is associated with hydrothorax
c. Is secondary to any GIT cancer
d. Shows characteristic mucoid epithelial change
e. None of the above
Answer:D : Krukenberg tumors are often characterized by mucin-secreting signet-ring cells in the tissue of the ovary .

124. CA-125 is ?
a. A mucin-type glycoprtein
b. A ganglioside
c. A tumor-specific transplantation antigen
d. Useful for ovarian cancer screening in the general patient population
e. An antigen which is commonly expressed by mucinous ovarian carcinomas

Answer: A: There is no screening test for ovarian epithelial cancers. CA 125 is a mucin-type glycoprotein which is usually not expressed by mucinous tumors. The antigen (CA 25) is expressed by fetal amniotic and coelomic epithelium. It is found in tissues derived from the coelmic epithelium (pericardium, pleura and peritoneum) and mullerian epithelium (tubal, endometrium and endocervical epithelium)

125. A 63 old lady presents with abdominal mass & weight loss , was diagnosed as having an ovarian tumor , the most common ovarian tumour in this woman would be...:
a. epithelial tumour
b. germ cell tumour
c. stromal tumour
d. sex cord tumour
e. trophoblastic tumour

Answer: A: Epithelial ovarian tumors are the commonest malignant neoplasms arising from the ovary and constitute almost 60-70 % of all ovarian cancers

126. A young female came to you with complaint of oligomenorrhea ,hirsutism & weight gain ,US reveals bulky ovaries with subcapsular cysts. Most likely diagnosis is
a. ovarian cancer
b. cushing syndrome
c. PCOD
d. DM
e. PID

Answer:C

127. A large cystic tumour is detected in a woman in routine antenatal examination. The most common complication she can encounter?
a. Torsion
b. rupture
c. hemorrhage
d. infection
e. degeneration

Answer:A

128. A 18-year-old woman comes to the physician for an annual examination. She has no complaints. She has been sexually active for the past 2 years. She uses the oral contraceptive pill for contraception. She has depression for which she takes fluoxetine. She takes no other medications and has no allergies to medications. Her family history is negative for cancer and cardiac disease. Examination is unremarkable.
Which of the following screening tests should this patient most likely have?
a. Colonoscopy
b. Mammogram
c. Pap smear
d. Pelvic ultrasound

e. Sigmoidoscopy
Answer:C : There is increased risk for cancer cervix due to the early age at the first sexual intercourse and also there is very small increase risk with OCPs use .So , Pap smear is the most likely to be done as a screening for cancer cervix .

131. Hilus or Leydig cell tumour may be associated with :
a. Reinke crystals
b. Oestrogen effect on endometrium
c. Clinical virilism
d. All of the above

e. None of the above

Answer:D : Reinke's crystals are rectangular, crystal-like inclusions in the interstitial cells of the testis (Leydig cells) and hilus cells in the ovary.

132. A multiparous woman aged 40 years, presents with menorahagia and progressively increasing dysmenorrhoea. Most probable diagnosis is:
a. Ca Cervix
b. Ca Endometrium
c. Adenomyosis
d. DUB

Answer:C

133. Female with history of frequent micturition may be :
a. prolapse
b. incarcerated fibroma
c. pregnancy
d. a&c
e. all above .

Answer:E

134. Considering dysgerminoma all true except :
a. the commonest germ cell tumor
b. usually in young females
c. lymphatic spread is so late
d. elevate lactic dehydrogenase level .
Answer:C: Dysgerminoma is more liable to early lymphatic spread to pelvic and para aortic node .

135. Ordering accord to the commonest cancers in female genital tract the right is :
a. cervical , endometrial ,ovarian

b. ovarian , cervical , endometrial
c. endometrial , cervical , ovarian
d. endometrial , ovarian , cervical .
Answer:C

136. Female came to the ER with Bp 80/60 and pulse 125 with history of acute abdomen , next step is
a. laparotomy
b. iv fluids
c. CBC
d. PV examination
Answer:B

137. Considering ovarian cancer :
a. surgery is preferred to be last line
b. early discovered with good prognosis
c. chemotherapy is good in most tumors
d. germ cell tumors show good response to chemotherapy
Answer:D

138. A 48-year-old woman has noted a small amount of irregular vaginal bleeding for the past 2 months. She has a pelvic examination that reveals no cervical lesions, and a Pap smear that shows no abnormal cells. Next, an endometrial biopsy is performed, and there is microscopic evidence for

endometrial hyperplasia. An abdominal ultrasound reveals a solid right ovarian mass. Which of the following neoplasms is this woman is most likely to have?

a. Mature cystic teratoma
b. Choriocarcinoma
c. Sertoli-Leydig cell tumor
d. Fibrothecoma
e. Krukenberg tumor
f. Cystadenocarcinoma

Answer: D

139. Vaginal adenocarcinomas in children is caused by

a. Virus
b. Administration of DES to pregnant mothers
c. Hormonal changes
d. All of the above

Answer: B

140. Carcinoma cervix with involvement of upper 2/3 of vagina is stage

a. II
b. II B
c. III A
d. III B

Answer: A

141. A 47-year-old woman has noted a pressure sensation, but no pain, in her pelvic region for the past 5 months. On physical examination there is a right adnexal mass. An ultrasound scan shows a 10 cm fluid-filled cystic mass in the right ovary. A fine needle aspirate of the mass is performed and cytologic examination of clear fluid aspirated from the mass reveals clusters of malignant epithelial cells surrounding psammoma bodies. Which of the following neoplasms is she most likely to have?

a. Endometrial adenocarcinoma
b. Ovarian serous cystadenocarcinoma
c. Mesothelioma
d. Ovarian mature cystic teratoma
e. Adenocarcinoma of fallopian tube

Answer: B

142. Ovarian masses:

a. Are malignant in presence of ascites
b. Include benign teratomas
c. Of germ cell origin may secrete hormones
d. May be confused with develpomental abnormalities of renal tract
e. If malignant can be reliably staged pre-operatively

Answer: B

143. A 4-year-old girl is noted to have breast enlargement and vaginal bleeding. On physical examination, she is noted to have a 9-cm pelvic mass. Which of the following is the most likely etiology?

a. Cystic teratoma
b. Dysgerminoma
c. Endodermal sinus tumor
d. Granulosa cell tumor
e. Mucinous tumor

Answer: D

144. Current modes of investigation for infertility to check functioning of tubes are all of the following execpt:

a. Air insufflation
b. Sonosalpingography
c. Hysterrosalpingography
d. Laparoscopic chromotubation
e. all of the above
Answer:E

145. Before puberty, what is the ratio between the cervical length and uterine body ?
a. 1 : 2
b. 2 : 1
c. 1 : 3
d. 1 : 4
Answer:B

146. As regard mastalgia:
a. in cyclic mastalgia pain is usaully max. postmenestrual
b. is treaeted surgically
c. bromocriptine may be used
d. gammaleinoliec acid is contraindicated
Answer:C

147. Pap smear
a. the next step in dysplastic smear is colposcopy
b. is simple but inaccurate
c. should be carried out every 5 years
d. has no role in screening of assymptomatic women
e. all of the above
Answer:A

148. A 40-years-old female with history of fibroid on investigation showed CIN-2 changes. Treatment of choice in this case is :
a. Hysterectomy
b. Conization
c. Cryotherapy
d. Laser ablation
Answer:A

149. Dysfunctional Uterine Bleeding (DUB) is defined as abnormal uterine bleeding ?
a. Secondary to hormonal dysfunction
b. Caused by cancer
c. In a patient with von Willebrand's disease

d. With no organic cause
e. Caused by an endometrial polyp
Answer:D

150. Abnormal Uterine bleeding (AUB) is defined by all of the following except ?
a. Excessive Blood loss (>80 ml) during menses
b. Menstrual length less than 7 days
c. An interval of less than 21 days between the starts of successive menses
d. Irregular bleeding episodes between menses
e. Extended (>35 days) intervals between menses
Answer:B

151. Dysfunctional uterine bleeding is said to present when there is bleeding due to :

a. Fibroid
b. Endometriosis
c. Irregular ripening and irregular shedding
d. Chronic endometritis
Answer:C

152. Post menopausal bleeding does not occur in....
a. Use of combined OCP's
b. Atrophic vaginitis
c. Endometrial hyperplasia
d. CA-Endometrium
Answer:A

153. Bicornute uterus may predispose to all the following except:
a. recurrent PTL
b. primary amenorrhea
c. retention of placenta after delivery
d. menorrhagia
Answer:B

PART-III

1. Which is the least frequent site of an ectopic pregnancy?
a. Fallopian tube
b. Cervix
c. Ovary
d. Abdominal cavity
e. Between the leaves of broad ligament
Answer: D: Fallopian Tubes:96% , Ovaries:2% & Cervix:<1%

2. Perforation tends to occur earliest when an ectopic pregnancy is located in which portion of fallopian tube ?
a. Isthmic
b. Interstitial
c. Ampullary
d. Infundibular
e. No difference
Answer:A: If the implantation is located in the narrow isthmic portion of the tube(the narrowest part), it will rupture very early, within 6 to 8 weeks; the distensible interstitial portion may be able to retain the pregnancy up to 14 weeks of gestation, while the ampulla is the widest portion.

3. Which of the following does not occur in post partum pituitary necrosis :
a. signs of hypoglycaemia
b. Asthenia
c. Amenorrhoea
d. Galactorrhoea
e. Decreased libido
Answer: C: failure of lactation occurs due to decreased prolactin secretion due to anterior pituitary insufficiency
- Hypoglycemia is due to 2ry adrenal insufficiency
- Amenorrhea and decreased libido are due to gonadotropin insufficiency
- Asthenia is the easy fatigability due to - GH >> -- muscle bulk

4. The most dangerous symptom during pregnancy is:
a. PV bleeding
b. Ankle swelling
c. Hyperemesis
d. Cramps

Answer:A

5. The Arius-Stella reaction may be seen with all except :
a. Ectopic pregnancy
b. Birth control pills
c. Abortion
d. Trophoblastic disease
Answer:B: Arius - Stella reaction is a benign change in the endometrium associated with the presence of chorionic tissue.

6. The passage of decidual cast in cases of ectopic pregnancy usually means :
a. Impending tubal rupture
b. Reabsorption of embryo
c. Pregnancy was intrauterine
d. Death of embryo

Answer:D

7. The following complications during pregnancy increase the risk of postpartum hemorrhage

(PPH) except:
a. Hypertension
b. Macrosomia
c. Twin pregnancy
d. Hydramnios
Answer:A: B, C, D: over distension of the uterus predisposes to atonic PPH

8. What is the most common side effect with MTX therapy for ectopic pregnancy
a. Transient pelvic pain 3 - 7 days after starting treatment
b. Stomatitis
c. Bone marrow suppression
d. Gastritis

Answer:B

9. Prenatal diagnosis at 16 weeks of pregnancy can be performed using all of the following, except:
a. Amniotic fluid
b. Maternal blood
c. Chorionic villi
d. Fetal blood

Answer:D

10. A primigravida presents to casualty at 32 weeks gestation with acute pain abdomen for 2 hours, vaginal bleeding and decreased fetal movements. She

should be managed by;
a. Immediate cesarean section
b. Immediate induction of labor
c. Tocolytic therapy
d. Magnesium sulphate therapy
Answer: A : Bleeding that affects the fetal condition(manifested here by fetal distress) is an indication of CS in Ante Partum Hemorrhage

11. Placenta previa, all true except :
a. Shock out of proportion of bleeding
b. Malpresentation
c. Head not engaged
d. Painless bleeding
Answer:A: Low lying placenta in the LUS interferes with normal adaptation of the fetal head to the female pelvis>>head is usually not engaged

12. A 34wk GA lady presented with vaginal bleeding of an amount more of that of her normal cycle. O/E uterine contracts every 4 min, bulged membrane, the cervix is 3 cm dilated, fetus is in a high transverse lie and the placenta is on the posterior fundus. US showed translucency behind the placenta and the CTG (Cardiotocography) showed FHR of 170, the best line of management is:
a. C/S immediately.
b. give oxytocin.
c. do rupture of the membrane.
d. amniocentisis

Answer:A

13. Most important cause of immediate post partum hemorrhage:
a. laceration of cervix

b. laceration of vagina
c. uterine atony
d. placental fragment retention

Answer:C

14. Factors favoring long anterior rotation include all except
a. Correction of the deflexion
b. Adequate pelvis
c. good pelvic floor
d. rupture of membranes
Answer: D : Adequate liquor is a factor favoring Long Anterior Rotation, not ROM

15. All following are indications for CS in OP except
a. Persistent oblique op
b. Long anterior rotation
c. Deep transverse arrest
d. Contracted pelvis
Answer: B : POP, DTA are obstructed and indications of CS
Long Anterior Rotation of the head is a good sign and the baby can be delivered vaginally

16. Which vitamin deficiency is most commonly seen in a pregnant mother who is on phenytoin therapy for epilepsy?
a. Vitamin B6
b. Vitamin B12
c. Vitamin A
d. Folic acid
Answer: D: Phenytoin inhibits the enzyme intestinal conjugase, an important enzyme in folic A. metabolism inside the body, thereby causing folate deficiency

17. Uterine inertia is due to EXCEPT?
a. Over distension of uterus
b. Presence of fibroid uterus
c. Fetal malpresentations
d. Abruptio placenta
e. repeated interautrine manipulation
Answer: D : as A, B, C, E predispose to hypotonic uterine inertia

18. Exposure of female fetus to androgens may arrest differentiation of :
a. Mullerian duct
b. Ovary
c. Urogenital sinus
d. All of the above
e. None of the above

Answer : C

19. The risk for development of fetal macrosomia is increased in the following, EXCEPT:
a. Primiparity.
b. Diabetes with pregnancy.
c. Post-term pregnancy.
d. Prior macrosomic infants.

Answer:A

20. Complications of the third stage of labor include all of the following except :

a. Rupture uterus.
b. Postpartum hemorrhage.
c. Puerperal sepsis.
d. Retained placenta.
e. Obstetric shock.

Answer:A

21. Shock is out of proportion to the amount of bleeding in :
a. 1ry postpartum haemorrhage
b. Retained placenta
c. Acute puerperal inversion of uterus
d. Hypofibrinogenemia
Answer:B: retention of the placenta > 2h. may cause shock even in absence of haemorrhage

22. The gold standard in diagnosing ectopic pregnancy
a. Laparoscopy
b. Culdocenteris
c. Beta HCG
d. US
e. Progesterone
Answer: A: The gold Standard in diagnosis of ectopic is not US alone Nor BhCG alone, rather a comiBnation of both:Absence of an intrauterine Gestational Sac + serum BhCG levels > the discriminatory zone is the GOLD STANDARD.

23. Which method of terminating a molar gestation is never indicated
a. Suction curettage
b. Prostaglandic
c. Hypertonicsaline
d. Hysterotomy
e. Hyterectomy

Answer: C

24. Invasive molar tissue is most commonly found in
a. Myometrium
b. Vaginal wall
c. Ovary
d. Liver
e. Lungs
Answer:A: Invasive molar tissue(locally invasive) invades the myometrium, while metastatic molar tissue (highly metsataic)is a different type which metastasizes to

the lung, liver... .

25. A 31-year-old, HIV-positive woman, gravida 3, para 2, at 32-weeks' gestation comes to the physician for a prenatal visit. Her prenatal course is significant for the fact that she has taken zidovudine throughout the pregnancy. Otherwise, her prenatal course has been unremarkable. She has no history of mental illness. She states that she has been weighing the benefits and risks of cesarean delivery in preventing transmission of the virus to her baby. After much deliberation, she has decided that she does not want a cesarean delivery and would like to attempt a vaginal delivery. Which of the following is the most appropriate next step in management?
a. Contact psychiatry to evaluate the patient
b. Contact the hospital lawyers to get a court order for cesarean delivery
c. Perform cesarean delivery at 38 weeks
d. Perform cesarean delivery once the patient is in labor

e. Respect the patient's decision and perform the vaginal delivery

Answer:E

26. A 19-year-old primigravid woman at 42 weeks' gestation comes the labor and delivery ward for induction of labor. Her prenatal course was uncomplicated. Examination shows her cervix to be long, thick, closed, and posterior. The fetal heart rate is in the 140s and reactive. The fetus is vertex on ultrasound. Prostaglandin (PGE2) gel is placed intravaginally. One hour later, the patient begins having contractions lasting longer than 2 minutes. The fetal heart rate falls to the 70s. Which of the following is the most appropriate next step in management?
a. Administer general anesthesia
b. Administer terbutaline
c. Perform amnioinfusion
d. Start oxytocin
e. Perform cesarean delivery
Answer:B: Quickly administer Terbutaline(Short Acting B2 Agonist) to decrease uterine contractility (fetal HR is steeply decreasing)

27. Which one of the following is a risk factor for developing DVT?
a. Family history of thromboembolic disease.
b. Factor V Leiden.
c. Antiphospholipid syndrome.
d. Sepsis.
e. All of the above.
Answer:E : Septic thrombophlebitis is a condition characterized by venous thrombosis,

inflammation, and bacteremia
(N.B.) : Factor V Leidenis the name given to a variant of human factor V that causes a hypercoagulability disorder

28. Pre-eclampsia.
a. is more common in women who have previously had a miscarriage.
b. is more common in women conceiving after oral contraception compared with women using barrier contraception.
c. is more common in women with a first degree relative who had PE.
d. regular full blood counts are helpful in monitoring the progress of the condition.
e. development of abdominal pain is a serious sign.
f. C,D&E

Answer:F

29. Premature labour.
a. is associated with an increased risk of breech presentation.
b. is associated with uterine anomaly.
c. asymptomaticbacteruria is a proven risk factor.
d. is associated with genital tract infection.
e. is associated with cigarette smoking.
f. All of the above

Answer:F

30. A 22-year-old woman in labor progresses to 7 cm dilation, and then has no further progress. She therefore undergoes a primary cesarean section. Examination 2 days after the section shows a temperature of 39.1 C (102.4 F), blood pressure of 110/70 mm Hg, pulse of 90/min, and respirations of 14/min. Lungs are clear to auscultation bilaterally. Her abdomen is moderately tender. The incision is clean, dry, and intact, with no evidence of erythema. Pelvic examination demonstrates uterine

tenderness. Which of the following is the most appropriate pharmacotherapy?
a. Ampicillin
b. Ampicillin-gentamicin
c. Clindamycin-gentamicin
d. Clindamycin-metronidazole
e. Metronidazole

Answer:D

31. A 19-year-old nulliparous woman in her 35th week of pregnancy presents with nausea, blurred vision and a weight gain of 4.5 kg per week. Her blood pressure is 160/110 mmHg. Which of the following tests is the most suitable for the

assessment of fetal status?
a. amniocentesis for the measurement of the lecithin/ sphingomyelin (L/S) ratio
b. amniocentesis for the measurement of the creatinine level of the amnotic fluid
c. sonographiccephalometry
d. a non-stress test (NST)
e. an oxytocin challenge test (OCT)

Answer:D

32. All of the following can be used in hypertension in Pregnancy except
a. Hydralazine
b. Labetolol
c. Captopril
d. Alpha methyl DOP
Answer: C : Captopril is a teratogenic that may cause abnormally small head , Neural tube defects , Heart defects, Underdeveloped lungs , Partial or complete absence of skull , etc
33. All are complications of illegal /Septic abortion except
a. Cerebral Hemorrhage
b. DIC
c. ARF
d. Bacterial Shock

Answer:A

34. A 31-year-old woman comes to the physician for follow-up after an abnormal Pap test and cervical biopsy. The patient's Pap test showed a high-grade squamous intraepithelial lesion (HGSIL). This was followed by colposcopy and biopsy of the cervix. The biopsy specimen also demonstrated HGSIL. The patient was counseled to undergo a loop electrosurgical excision procedure (LEEP). Which of the following represents the potential long-term complications from this procedure?
a. Abscess and chronic pelvic inflammatory disease
b. Cervical incompetence and cervical stenosis
c. Constipation and fecal incontinence
d. Hernia and intraperitoneal adhesions
e. Urinary incontinence and urinary retention
Answer:B

35. Female patient with history of irregular vaginal bleeding tender right iliac fossa , CBC normal , B-HCG positive , most likely to be :
a. corpus luteum cyst
b. appendicitis

c. ectopic pregnancy
d. none of the above

Answer:C: corpus luteum cysts and appendicitis don't show ++ B-hCG .

36. Cervical lesion (ectopy):
a. It is an ulcer of the cervix.
b. Should be treated in pregnant females.
c. Pap smear is advisable before management.
d. Commonly cause pain, dyspareunia & low back pain.
Answer:D

37. Engagement all true except :
a. the biparietal diameter in the pelvic inlet
b. grasped by 1st pelvic grip
c. at the onset of labor in multiparas
d. Preferring an empty bladder.
Answer:B : 1st pelvic grip is for detection of the presentingpart, while 2nd pelvic grip is to detect its engagement

38. The foetal well-being can be assessed by all of the following, except ?
a. non-stress test
b. contraction stress test
c. ultrasound
d. oxytocin sensitivity test!!!
Answer:D

39. In which of the following condition vaginal delivery is contraindicated?
a. Extended breech
b. Mento anterior
c. Twins with one vertex and one breech
Answer: A: Breech with extended legs: frank breech is an indication of CS

40. Which is contraindicated in trial of labour following Caesarian Section ?
a. History of Classical CS
b. Breech
c. X-ray pelivmetry not available
d. No previous vaginal delivery
Answer:B

41. A 20 year old full-term primigravida is brought to the casualty with labour pains for last 24 hours and a hand prolapse. On examination, she has pulse 96/min, BP

120/80 mm Hg, and mild pallor. The abdominal examination reveals the uterine height at 32 weeks, the foetus in transverse lie and absent foetal heart sounds. On vaginal examination, the left arm of the foetus is prolapsed and the foetal ribs are palpable. The pelvis is adequate. What would be the best management option ?
a. External cephalic version
b. Decapitation and delivering the baby vaginally
c. Internal podalic version
d. Lower Segment Caesarean section
Answer: B:Because absent Fetal heart Sounds = Dead baby! >> Decapitation and delver vaginally

42. Which one of the following is diagnosed by Spiegelberg criteria ?
a. Molar pregnancy
b. Ovarian pregnancy
c. Uterine pregnancy
d. Twin pregnancy Answer: B :
Spiegelberg criteria is used to diagnose Ovarian ectopic : via laparotomy/ laparoscopy Four criteria

for differentiating ovarian from other ectopic pregnancies:
1) The gestational sac is located in the region of the ovary.
2) The ectopic pregnancy is attached to the uterus by the ovarian ligament.
3) Ovarian tissue in the wall of the gestational sac is proved histologically.
4) The tube on the involved side is intact.

43. The presence of a retraction ring at the junction of upper and lower uterine segment in labour indicates ?
a. Prolonged labour
b. Cervical dystocia
c. Obstructed labour
d. Precipitate labour

Answer:C

44. The indications of an elective caesarean section include all of the following, except ?
a. Placenta Praevia
b. Cephalopelvic disproportion
c. Previous lower segment caesarean section
d. Carcinoma Cervix
Answer:C : isn't it supposed to be cancer Cervix?? Previous CS IS an indication of elective CS!

45. Hyperemesis gravidarium in 1st trimester is seen with increased frequency in all of the following except:
a. H. Mole
b. Twins
c. Pre-eclampsia
d. Primigravida
Answer:C: H. mole and multifetal pregnancies++ risk of HEG because ++++ BhCG Primigravidas are more prone to HEG

46. Most common indication for C/S :
a. malpresentations
b. antepartum hge
c. prematurity
d. previous c/s
e. contracted pelvis
Answer:D

47. Which of the follwing is responsible for inability to rotate anteriorly in the occipitoposterior position :
a. Moderate size fetus
b. Gynecoid pelvis
c. Weak uterine contractions
d. Good levatorani muscle contractions

Answer:C

48. Ectopic pregnancy is differentiated from abortion by the fact that in ectopic pregnancy :
a. Pain appears after vaginal bleeding
b. There is slight amount of bleeding
c. No enlargement of uterus
d. Histological examination of products of expulsion shows villi

Answer:D

49. Following a vaginal delivery, a woman develops a fever, lower abdominal pain and uterine tenderness. She is alert, and her blood pressure and urine output are good. Large gram positive rods suggestive of clostridia are seen in a smear of cervix. management should include all except :

a. Immediate radiographic examination for gas in uterus
b. High dose antibiotic therapy
c. Hysterectomy

d. close observation for renal failure or hemolysis Answer:C : Clostridia are anerobic gas producing organisms

50. Engaging diameter, in fully extended head :

a. Mento occipital
b. Submentobregmatic
c. Biparietal
d. Mentovertica

Answer:B: SubmentoBregmatic = 9.5 cm in fully extended = face presentation

51. A woman experiencing a molar pregnancy has an increased risk of which of the following in subsequent gestations?

a. Stillbirth
b. Prematurity
c. Congenital malformations
d. Recurrent molar gestation
e. Cancer later in life

Answer: D: Recurrence rate is 1-2% in next gestations

52. A woman with a complete mole is most likely to present with which of the symptoms?

a. Vaginal Bleeding
b. Excessive uterine size
c. Hypermesis
d. Prominent theca lutein cysts
e. Pre-eclampsia

Answer: A: Recurrent mild vaginal bleeding is the most common presenting symptom in the 1st trimester.

53. Fetal hyperinsulinemia leads to:

a. Fetal macrosomia causes difficult vaginal delivery
b. Inhibition of pulmonary surfactant causing Intrauterine asphyxia
c. Decrease serum K causing respiratory distress syndrome
d. Neonatal hypoglycemia with myocardial injury

Answer: A: Fetal hyperglycemia>>hyperinsulinemia>>macrosomia due to :insulin++ lipogenesis and glycogenesis, ptn synthesis (anabolic hormone)

54. The following are eitiological factors of atonic postpartum hge except :

a. prolonged labour
b. overdistension of uterus
c. full bladder

d. cervical lacerations
e. accidental he .

Answer: D: Cervical lacerations are a cause of PPH , but not the atonic type

55. If the foetus is lying accros the uterus, with the head in the flank

a. Transverse lie
b. Cephalic lie
c. Breech lie

d. Frank lie
e. Oblique lie

Answer:A

56. Refers to the part of the foetus that occupies the lower segment of the uterus or pelvic
a. The show
b. The version
c. The engagement
d. The lie
e. The presentation

Answer:E

57. Means the head is at the level of the ischial spines
a. Station +1
b. Station -1
c. Station -2
d. Station 0
e. Station +2

Answer:D

58. Engagement is said to occur when.......
a. The fetal head is within the maternal pelvis
b. The biparietal diameter of the fetal head is through the plane of the inlet.
c. The presenting part is just above the level of ischial spines.
d. The vertex is in transverse position Answer:B

59. The following hormone is not produced by the placenta...
a. HCG
b. HPL
c. Prolactin
d. Estriol

Answer:C

60. Which is the most common cause of abnormal lie?
a. Polyhydramnios
b. Twin pregnancy
c. Uterine deformity
d. Pelvic tumour
e. Placenta praevia

Answer: A

61. Which of the following statements regarding vaginal breech birth is FALSE?
a. Increased risk if footling
b. In about 30% there is slow cervical dilatation in the first stage
c. CTG is advised
d. Pushing is not encouraged until the buttocks are visible
e. Epidural analgesia is mandatory

Answer:E

62. Refers to a maneuver which attempts to turn a breech baby to a cephalic presentation

a. VEC
b. CEV
c. ECR
d. EVC
e. ECV

Answer:E

63. Refers to the part of the foetus that occupies the lower segment of the uterus or pelvis
a. The show
b. The version
c. The engagement
d. The lie
e. The presentation

Answer:E

64. Engagement is said to occur when.......
a. The fetal head is within the maternal pelvis
b. The biparietal diameter of the fetal head is through the plane of the inlet.
c. The presenting part is just above the level of ischial spines.
d. The vertex is in transverse position.

Answer:B

65. After what age gestation would abnormal lie warrant hospital admission
a. 37
b. 40
c. 38
d. 39
e. 36

Answer:A

66. The most common type of breech
a. Starling breech
b. Flexed breech
c. Explicit breech
d. Footling breech
e. Extended breech
Answer:E : Extended breech= Breech with extended legs

67. At which part of the pelvis are the transverse and anterior-posterior diameter most similar?
a. Inlet
b. Mid-cavity
c. Outlet Answer:B

68. Breech presentations occurs in _ of term pregnancies
a. 1%
b. 3%
c. 8%
d. 4-10%
e. 5-6%
Answer:B : Percentage significantly increases in the preterm ..may reach up to 25%

69. Flexion of the fetal head occurs when it meets resistance from :

a. Pelvic floor
b. Cervix
c. Pelvic walls
d. Any of the above
e. None of the above
Answer:A

70. A woman delivers a 9 lb baby with midline episiotomy & develops a 3rd degree tear. Inspection shows that the following structures are intact.
a. Anal sphincter
b. Perineal body
c. Rectal mucosa
d. Perineal muscles
Answer:C: in third degree tears all are injured except. Rectal mucosa 9 lb. mean 9 pounds which is the method of calculating weight abroad

71. Leopold maneuvers refers to :
a. delivery of head
b. External version
c. Internal version
d. Breech extraction
e. Examination of abdomen.
Answer:E: Leopold's Maneuvers = Fundal Grip, Pelvic Grips (1st&2nd), Umbilical Grip, Pawlick's Grip.

72. Following changes occur in urinary system during normal pregnancy:
a. Increase in renal blood flow
b. Increase in glomerular filtration rate
c. Increase in capacity of kidney pelvis
d. All of the above
Answer:D: The well-known dilation of the ureters and renal pelvis begins by the second month of pregnancy and is maximal by the middle of the second trimester,

73. Mechanism of labor in abortion stick (use of stick to induce abortion)is due to
a. Necrosis of uterine endometrium and stimulation of uterine contraction
b. Oxytocin present in the stick
c. Prostaglandins present in the stick
d. All of the above
Answer:A

PART IV

1. In three tier system of CTG interpretation, category III abnormalCTG is all EXCEPT

a. Absent baseline FHR variability and recurrent late deceleration
b. Absent baseline FHR variability and recurrent variable deceleration
c. Absent baseline FHR variability and bradycardia
d. Prolonged deceleration > 2 min but < 10 min
Answer: d

2. Absolute contraindications to neuraxial analgesia in labour includeall EXCEPT

a. Maternal coagulopathy
b. Thrombocytopenia
c. Prophylactic low-molecular-weight heparin within 12 hours
d. Refractory maternal hypertension
Answer: d

3. Proven contraindications for the use of PGE2 for induction oflabour include all EXCEPT

a. suspicion of fetal compromise
b. bronchial asthma
c. unexplained vaginal bleeding
d. cephalopelvic disproportion
Answer: b

4. McRobert's maneuver for relieving shoulder dystocia acts by all thefollowing EXCEPT

a. straightening of the sacrum relative to the lumbar vertebrae
b. rotation of the symphysis pubis toward the maternal head
c. decrease in the angle of pelvic inclination
d. increase in overall pelvic dimensions
Answer: d

5. All the following statements are TRUE EXCEPT

a. Case-control studies are most feasible for examining the association between arelatively common exposure and a relatively rare disease
b. Strengths of cohort studies include the ability to obtain attributable and relativerisks (RRs) because the occurrence of the outcome is being compared in twogroups
c. Phase 3 clinical trials determine the efficacy of treatment for the intendedpopulation, compared with other available treatments, assess adverse events andside effects
d. The negative predictive value (NPV) and positive predictive value (PPV) of atest does not vary with the baseline characteristics of population or prevalence ofa disease
Answer: d

6. The FALSE statement regarding trichomonial vaginitis is

a. Increased risk of PPROM and PTL in pregnant women and higher posthysterectomy cuff infection
b. Less than 10% of men contract the disease after a single exposure to an infectedwoman
c. T. vaginalis infection is associated with a two to three fold increased risk forHIV acquisition
d. Clue cells and Whiff test may be positive in TV
Answer: b

7. Find the FALSE statement regarding cervicitis

a. The microbial etiology of endocervicitis is unknown in about 50% of cases inwhich neither gonococci nor chlamydia is detected
b. Mycoplasma genitaliem, can be detected in 10% to 30% of women with clinicalcervicitis
c. Nucleic acid amplification tests (NAAT) for gonorrhea and chlamydia, is notmandatory in all cases
d. Cervicitis is commonly associated with BV, which if not treated concurrently,leads to significant persistence
Answer: c

8. All the statements regarding PID are TRUE EXCEPT

a. About 75% of women with tubo-ovarian abscess do not respond toantimicrobial therapy alone and need drainage
b. No definite symptoms are defined to diagnose PID

c. Evaluation of both vaginal and endocervical secretions is a crucial part of theworkup of a patient with PID
d. Additional criteria to increase the specificity of the diagnosis includeendometrial biopsy, CRP and positive test for gonorrhea or chlamydia andlaparoscopy
Answer: a

9. Regarding genital ulcers find the TRUE statement
a. The ulcer of syphilis has irregular margins and is deep with undermined edges
b. The chancroid ulcer has a smooth, indurated border and a smooth base
c. The genital herpes ulcer is often multiple, sub-epidermal and inflamed
d. If inguinal buboes with no ulcer is present, the most likely diagnosis is LGV
Answer: d

10. Regarding testing in genital ulcers which of the followingstatements is FALSE
a. (VDRL) test and a confirmatory treponemal test – fluorescent treponemalantibody absorption (FTA ABS) or microhemagglutinin-T. pallidum should beused to diagnose syphilis presumptively in all cases
b. HSV culture sensitivity approaches 100% in the vesicle stage but PCR assays forHSV DNA are more sensitive in the ulcerative stage
c. Optimally, the evaluation of a patient with a genital ulcer should include culturefor Haemophilusducreyi
d. The diagnosis remains unconfirmed in more than half of patients (60%) withgenital ulcers
Answer: d

11. Medical management of endometriosis – Find the FALSEstatement
a. Approximately 85% of women with endometriosis and pelvic pain who aretreated with GnRH agonists experience relief of their pain
b. Dienogest is effective in improving endometriosis-associated pain and mayeven help overcome progesterone resistance by increasing the number ofprogesterone receptors
c. Estrogen-progestin contraceptives is cytoreductive and halts progression ofendometriosis in upto 90% of affected women when taken continuously
d. The levonorgestrel-releasing intrauterine device is of value in women with deepinfiltrating rectovaginal endometriosis in reducing pain and dysmenorrhearecurrence following surgical therapy
Answer: c

12. Find the INCORRECT statement regarding Ectopic pregnancy
a. the overall risk of recurrence is approximately 10% for women with oneprevious ectopic pregnancy and at least 25% for women having two or more
b. estrogen-progestin contraceptives and vasectomy are associated with the lowestabsolute incidence of ectopic pregnancy (0.005 ectopic pregnancies/1,000 womenyears)
c. if pregnancy does occur with an IUD in situ, the risk for ectopic pregnancy is ashigh as 80%
d. approximately one-third of all pregnancies resulting from sterilization failureare ectopic
Answer: c

13. Medical Management of Ectopic pregancy-Find INCORRECTstatement
a. In 85% cases, serum β-hCG concentrations rise somewhat between days 1 and 4and does not necessarily indicate failed treatment
b. Medical treatment is not contraindicated for ectopic pregnancies with serum β-hCG concentrations greater than 5,000 IU/L or presence of embryonic heartactivity, but the likelihood of treatment failure and the risk of tubal rupture areincreased substantially
c. Anti D immunoglobulin need be administered only tononsensitized Rh-negative women with ectopic pregnancy undergoing surgical management
d. Free peritoneal fluid may be observed in almost 40% of women with earlyunruptured ectopic pregnancies and that the presence or absence of cul-de-sacfluid does not accurately predict the success or failure of medical treatment
Answer: c

14. Fetoplacental blood volume at term is approximately
a. 125 ml/kg of fetal weight
b. 80 ml/kg of fetal weight
c. 45 ml/kg of fetal weight
d. 240 ml/kg of fetal weight

Answer: a

15. Find the INCORRECT statement regarding internationalguidelines on vaccination in pregnancy

a. A dose of tetanus-diphtheria-acellular pertussis (Tdap) is ideally given togravidas between 27 and 36 weeks' gestation
b. All women who will be pregnant during influenza season should be offeredvaccination, regardless of gestational age
c. Avoid becoming pregnant for atleast one month after MMR vaccination
d. HPV vaccination may be administered to high risk pregnant women after thefirst trimester of pregnancy
Answer: d

16. The FALSE statement regarding fetal biometry by USS is

a. Until 14 weeks' gestation, the Crown-Rump Length (CRL) is accurate to within5 to 7 days
b. The biparietal diameter (BPD) most accurately reflects gestational age, with avariation of 7 to 10 days in the second trimester
c. If the head shape is flattened-dolichocephaly or rounded brachycephaly, theHead Circumference (HC) is more reliable than the BPD
d. To measure the AC, a circle is placed outside the fetal skin in a transverse imagethat contains the stomach, the kidneys and the confluence of the umbilical veinwith the portal sinus
Answer: d

17. All the following are indications for fetal ECHO EXCEPT

a. thick nuchal translucency
b. monochorionic twin gestation
c. maternal anti cardiolipin antibodies
d. maternal pregestational diabetes orphenylketonuria
Answer: c

18. Fetal renal pelviectasis – Find the CORRECT statement

a. is present in 20 to 30 percent of fetuses
b. in 30 percent of cases, it is transient or physiological
c. the pelvis is typically considered dilated if it exceeds 4 mm in the secondtrimester or 7 mm at approximately 32 weeks' gestation
d. mild pyelectasis in the second trimester is not considered a soft marker fordown syndrome
Answer: c

19. All the statements about Hydramnios (Polyhydramnios) are TRUEEXCEPT

a. it is diagnosed when AFI exceeds 24 and complicates 1 to 2 percent of singletonpregnancies
b. underlying causes of hydramnios include fetal anomalies-in approximately 15percent and diabetes in 15 to 20 percent
c. the degree of hydramnios correlates with the likelihood of an anomalous infant
d. idiopathic hydramnios accounts for upto 30 percent of cases of hydramnios
Answer: d

20. Find the FALSE statement regarding teratogens in pregnancy

a. less than 1 percent of all birth defects are caused by medications
b. 80 percent of birth defects do not have an obvious etiology and of those withanidentified cause, nearly 95 percent of cases have chromosomal or genetic origins
c. mono therapy with Levitracetam is associated with a 8-percent majormalformation rate, which is slightly higher than that for the general population
d. sulfonamides and nitrofurantoin are appropriate for use in pregnancy only ifsuitable alternatives are lacking
Answer: c

21. The following structures may be injured during sacrospinousligament fixation EXCEPT

a. Pudendal nerve
b. Superior gluteal artery
c. Inferior gluteal artery
d. Internal pudendal vessels
Answer: b

22. All the following statements about ureteric injury are TRUEEXCEPT

a. 75% of all iatrogenic injuries to the ureter result from gynecologic procedures
b. Laparoscopic hysterectomies have the least rate of ureteral injuries and vaginalhysterectomies the highest
c. Ninety-one percent of injuries occur at the level of the pelvicureter and only 2%and 7% occur at the upper and middle ureteral thirds
d. Careful identification of the ureter before securing the infundibulopelvicligament and uterine artery is the best protection against ureteric injury duringhysterectomy
Answer: b

23. All are TRUE regarding Dermoid cysts of ovary EXCEPT
a. Malignant transformation occurs in less than 2% of dermoid cysts in women ofall ages
b. Upto 25% of dermoids occur in postmenopausal women
c. The risk of torsion with dermoid cysts is approximately 50%
d. They are bilateral in approximately 10% of cases
Answer: c

24. All are TRUE regarding Endometrial Intraepithelial Neoplasia(EIN) EXCEPT
a. Approximately 40% to 50% of women with atypical hyperplasia or EIN haveconcurrent carcinoma
b. The risk of progression of hyperplasia without atypia to cancer is low but isapproximately 30% among those with atypical hyperplasia
c. Infertile women with EIN treated with high dose progestins should have anendometrial biopsy every 3 months
d. For women with EIN treated with progestins, recurrence risks approach 10%
Answer: d

25. According to the FIGO fibroid classification system type 3 is
a. 50% or more of the fibroid diameter within the myometrium
b. Intramural and entirely within the myometrium, without extension to eitherthe endometrial surface or to the serosa
c. Abuts the endometrium without any intracavitary component
d. Located in cervix or broad ligament
Answer: c

26. All are TRUE about atypical leiomyomas EXCEPT
a. Mitotically active leiomyoma is defined by the presence of 5 to 10 mitoses/10high-power fields and may be found in pregnancy and OCP users
b. Cellular leiomyomas exhibiting chromosome 1p deletions, may be clinicallymore aggressive
c. STUMP shows atypical histologic features that range between leiomyoma andLMS but the mitotic count is less than 10/10 hpf
d. STUMP mostly those that are p53 and p16 positive, have been found to exhibitmalignant potential to develop a low-grade LMS
Answer: a

27. Contraindications to Uterine Artery Embolisation (UAE) includeall EXCEPT
a. desirous of future fertility
b. impaired renal dysfunction
c. diminished immune status
d. willingness for hysterectomy
Answer: d

28. The pharmacologic treatments for vulvodynia can include topicallidocaine 5% with any of the following EXCEPT
a. oral gabapentine and steroids
b. botulinum toxin injections
c. combined oestrogen and progesterone pills
d. menopausal hormone therapy
Answer: c

29. Find the INCORRECT statement about Chronic Pelvic Pain (CPP)
a. There appears to be no relationship between the incidence and severity of painor the stage of the endometriotic lesions
b. The specific location and density of pelvic adhesions correlates consistentlywith the presence of pain symptoms

c. Endometriosis can be demonstrated in 15% to 40% of patients undergoinglaparoscopy for CPP
d. The accuracy of ultrasound in detecting ovarian remnant syndrome can beimproved by treating the patient with a 5- to 10-day course of clomiphene citrate
Answer: b

30. Find the FALSE statement regarding elagolix
a. used to suppress the estrogen production to a level that is adequate forsymptom relief but minimizes hypoestrogenic effects
b. cannot produce a dose-dependent suppression of pituitary function and ovarianhormones like GnRH agonists
c. improves dysmenorrhea and nonmenstrual pelvic pain during a 6-monthperiod in women with endometriosis-associated pain
d. orally active GnRH antagonist with no flare effect
Answer: b

31. All are TRUE regarding serous borderline ovarian tumoursEXCEPT
a. 10% of all ovarian serous tumors are of borderline type and 50% occur beforethe age of 40 years
b. Up to 40% of serous borderline tumors are associated with spread beyond theovary
c. Up to 10% of women with ovarian serous borderline tumors and extraovarianimplants may have invasive implants
d. Borderline serous tumors may harbor foci of stromal microinvasion and if so,should be managed as aggressive serous carcinomas
Answer: d

32. In Kyoto (Querlou and Morrow) classification, Nerve sparingRadical Hysterectomy is
a. Type B
b. Type C1
c. Type C2
d. Type D2
Answer: b

33. All are TRUE about Germ cell tumours EXCEPT
a. In patients with stage IA dysgerminoma, unilateral oophorectomy alone resultsin a 5-year disease-free survival rate of greater than 95%
b. Patients with stage IA, grade 1 immature teratoma need 4 cycles of BEPadjuvant therapy after surgery
c. All patients with Endodermal Stromal Tumours (EST) should be treated withchemotherapy shortly after recovering from surgery ovarian dysfunction of failure
d. Transient ovarian failure is common with platinum-based chemotherapy forgerm cell tumours and majority will have successful childbearing in the future
Answer: b

34. All the following statements regarding Granulosa cell tumours ofthe ovary are TRUE EXCEPT
a. Endometrial cancer occurs in association with granulosa cell tumors in at least5% of cases
b. 25-50% of Granulosa cell tumours are associated with endometrial hyperplasia
c. Granulosa cell tumors may also produce androgens and cause virilization
d. Juvenile granulosa cell tumors of the ovary are rare and behaves moreaggressively than the adult type
Answer: d

35. All the following statements about intrahepatic cholestasis ofpregnancy are TRUE EXCEPT
a. bile acids are cleared incompletely and accumulate in plasma but the cause isunclear
b. pruritus shows predilection for the soles and may precede laboratory findingsby several weeks
c. total plasma concentrations of bilirubin exceed 8 mg/dL and serumtransaminases exceed 500 in 30% patients
d. ursodeoxycholic acid relieves pruritus and improves fetal outcome better thansteroids and cholestyramine
Answer: c

36. All the statements about sickle cell anaemia in pregnancy areTRUE EXCEPT
a. Sickle-cell trait does not appear to be associated with increased perinatalmortality, low birthweight

or pregnancy-induced hypertension
b. In Sickle cell disease there is no categorical contraindication to vaginal delivery,and caesarean delivery is reserved for obstetrical indications
c. Routine prophylactic blood transfusions during labour is recommended toreduce painful crises in Sickle cell anaemia
d. Antenatal folic acid supplementation with 4 mg daily throughout pregnancy isneeded to support rapid red blood cell turnover
Answer: c

37. All the statements about thrombocytopenia in pregnancy areTRUE EXCEPT
a. A platelet count of < 80,000/L should trigger an evaluation for etiologies otherthan gestational thrombocytopenia
b. Hypertensive disorders account for 21% of thrombocytopenia in pregnancy
c. In ITP complicating pregnancy, therapy with steroids is considered if theplatelet count is below 30,000 to 50,000/L
d. Maternal platelet counts have strong correlation with fetal platelet counts andcaesarean delivery is recommended if platelet count is < 50,000 on fetal bloodsampling
Answer: d

38. All the following statements regarding diabetes in pregnancy areTRUE EXCEPT
a. Periconceptional HbA1C should be kept under 6.5% in pregestational diabeticwomen
b. MSAFP levels may be lower in diabetic pregnancies and the incidence ofcongenital cardiac anomalies is five fold in mothers with diabetes
c. Ultra short acting insulin analogues starts acting in 30 minutes, peaks in 2 hrsminutes and is good for preprandial glycemic control in pregnancy
d. Insulin therapy is typically added if fasting levels persistently exceed 95 mg/dLafter medical nutrition therapy
Answer: c

39. All the statements about thyroid in pregnancy are TRUE EXCEPT
a. Women with TPO antibodies are at increased risk for progression of thyroiddisease and postpartum thyroiditis
b. It is recommended that women avoid pregnancy for 1 month after radioablativetherapy with iodine 131
c. Pregnancy is associated with an increased thyroxine requirement inapproximately a third of supplemented women
d. Prophylthiouracil (PTU) is preferred in pregnancy because it partially inhibitsthe conversion of T4 to T3 and crosses the placenta less readily than methimazole
Answer: b

40. All the statements about SLE in pregnancy are TRUE EXCEPT
a. Fetal cell micro chimerism leads to the predilection for autoimmune disorderslike SLE among women
b. In the presence of anti-Ro and Anti-La antibodies, the incidence of fetalmyocarditis and heart block is as high as 20%
c. During pregnancy, lupus improves in a third of women, remains unchanged in athird and worsens in the remaining third
d. Hydroxychloroquine is not associated with congenital malformations and canbe continued in pregnancy
Answer: b

41. Identify the FALSE statement regarding Test for Ovarian Reserve
a. Total number of antral follicles measuring 2-10 mm in both ovaries isproportional to the number of primordial follicles remaining
b. Small antral follicles (2-6 mm) are likely the primary source of AMH becausethey contain larger numbers of granulosa cells and a more developedmicrovasculature
c. Recent studies suggest AMH levels decrease with the use of oral contraceptivesand GnRH agonists
d. A single elevated Day -3 FSH concentration (>10 IU/L) has high specificity forpredicting poor response to stimulation or failure to achieve pregnancy
Answer: d

42. Find the FALSE statement

a. The prevalence of uterine anomalies in infertile women and fertile women withnormal reproductive outcomes is similar, approximately 2-4%
b. Submucousmyomas reduce IVF success rates by approximately 70% andintramural myomas by approximately 20-40%
c. Hysteroscopic polypectomy may improve reproductive performance in infertilewomen
d. Conception and term delivery rates after successful hysteroscopiclysis ofintrauterine adhesions are > 80%
Answer: d

43. The FALSE statement regarding Male infertility is
a. 2-5% of men with severe oligospermia and 8% of men with azoospermia mayhave Y chromosome microdeletions
b. Hyperprolactinemia and treatment with GnRH analogs or androgens can causehypogonadotropic hypogonadism in males
c. Men with idiopathic infertility have significantly lesser CAG trinucleotide repeatlengths in androgen receptor gene
d. Disorders of estrogen synthesis or action may be associated with infertility inmen
Answer: c

44. Risk factors for Ovarian Hyperstimulation Syndrome (OHSS)include all EXCEPT
a. Young age
b. Higher BMI
c. Higher AMH and AFC
d. Higher serum Oestradiol
Answer: b

45. Preimplantation Genetic Testing (PGT) – Find the FALSEstatement
a. Can be used to detect numerical chromosomal aneuploidies and monogenicdisorders but not structural rearrangements
b. Chromosomal composition of the oocyte may be inferred from that of theextruded polar bodies
c. One or two blastomeres may be removed from cleavage stage embryos
d. Biopsy of the trophectoderm can be performed at the blastocyst stage and hasbecome the most commonly used technique
Answer: a

46. All are TRUE regarding cell free fetal DNA EXCEPT
a. Reliably detected in maternal blood after 9 to 10 weeks' gestation
b. The proportion of cell-free DNA that is placental is called the fetal fraction andit composes approximately 50 percent of the total circulating cell-free DNA inmaternal plasma
c. The specificity to detect down syndrome, trisomy 18 and trisomy 13 is over 99percent
d. Real-time quantitative polymerase chain reaction (PCR) may be used for Rhgenotyping, detection of paternally inherited single-gene disorders or fetal sexdetermination
Answer: b

47. All are TRUE regarding Prenatal Diagnosis EXCEPT
a. Biopsy of chorionic villi is typically performed between 10 and 13 weeks'gestation
b. Transabdominal amniocentesis is generally done between 11 and 14 weeks
c. FISH studies are usually completed within 24 to 48 hours
d. Chromosomal MicroArray can often be performed directly on unculturedamniocytes with a turn around time of only 3 to 5 days
Answer: b

48. All are TRUE regarding Anti D immunoglobulin EXCEPT
a. 300 mcg dose is given for each 15 mL of fetal red cells or 30 mL of fetal wholeblood to be neutralized
b. Anti-D immune globulin may produce a weakly positive-1 : 1 to 1 : 4-indirectcoombs titer in the mother
c. Routine postpartum administration of anti-D immune globulin to at-riskpregnancies within 72 hours of delivery lowers the alloimmunization rate by 50percent
d. Antepartum anti-D immune globulin at 28 weeks' gestation reduces the third-trimester alloimmunization rate from approximately 2 percent to 0.1 percent
Answer: c

49. All are TRUE regarding Non-Stress Test NST EXCEPT
a. Before 32 weeks, normal accelerations are defined as having an acme that is 10bpm or more above baseline for 10 seconds or longer
b. Beat-to-beat variability is under the control of the autonomic nervous system
c. Loss of reactivity is most commonly associated with fetal hypoxia
d. Abnormal non-stress test is inadequate to preclude any acuteasphyxial eventhappening in a 7 day interval
Answer: c
50. All are TRUE regarding miscarriage EXCEPT
a. balanced structural chromosomal rearrangements may originate from eitherparent and are found in 2 to 4 percent of couples with recurrent pregnancy loss
b. the incidence of euploid abortion rises dramatically after maternal age exceeds35 years
c. a threshold CRL of 5 mm with absent cardiac activity is used to diagnose non-viability or embryonic demise
d. absence of an embryo in a sac with a mean sac diameter (MSD) 25 mm signifiesan embryonic pregnancy
Answer: c
51. All are TRUE statements regarding female sterilisation in IndiaEXCEPT
a. Laparoscopic tubal ligation can be done concurrently with second-trimesterabortion and in the post-partum period only by an expert operator
b. The consent of the spouse is not required for sterilization
c. Clients should be married with female client below the age of 49 years andabove the age of 22 years
d. The couple need have minimum one child whose age is above one year unlessthe sterilization is medically indicated
Answer: a
52. All the following statements are TRUE EXCEPT
a. BMI greater than 35 or weight greater than 100 kg, should receive 2 g ofcefazolin as preoperative antibiotic prophylaxis
b. In as many as 50% of postoperative patients, Febrile morbidity in first 48 hoursis noninfectious and does not need antibiotics
c. Even a single dose of perioperative prophylactic antibiotic decreases theincidence of postoperative urinary tract infection from 40% to as low as 4%
d. Incidence of wound infections could be decreased by hexachlorophene showersbefore surgery and shaving of the woundsite just prior to incision
Answer: d
53. All the following are TRUE about Enhanced Recovery-ERASProtocol EXCEPT
a. Preoperative carbohydrate loading
b. The use of liberal antiemetics including preoperative steroids
c. Avoiding routine nasogastric tube and drains
d. Adequate pain relief with opiods
Answer: d
54. Find the CORRECT statement regarding laparoscopy.
a. To avoid injury to the deep inferior epigastric vessels, the lateral trocar shouldbe placed 3 to 4 cm medial to the medial umbilical ligament
b. Transillumination of the abdominal wall from within permits the identificationof the deep inferior epigastric vessels in most thin women
c. The amount of gas transmitted into the peritoneal cavity should depend on themeasured intraperitoneal pressure, not the volume of gas inflated
d. Hasson's open entry method is better than the closed method in preventingorgan injury
Answer: c
55. Find the FALSE statement.
a. Data are insufficient regarding fasting times for clear liquids and the risk ofpulmonary aspiration during labor
b. Modest amounts of clear liquids can be allowed in uncomplicated laboringwomen
c. Obvious solid foods are best avoided

d. A fasting period of 6 to 8 hours for solid food is recommended foruncomplicated parturients prior to undergoing Category I, II and III Caesareansections
Answer: d

56. Findings consistent with an Acute Peripartum or intrapartumevent leading to Hypoxic-Ischemic Encephalopathy are the followingEXCEPT

a. Apgar score < 5 at 5 and 10 minutes
b. Umbilical arterial pH < 7.0 and/or base deficit > 12 mmo I/L
c. Sentinel hypoxic or ischemic event occurring immediately before or duringdelivery
d. Spastic diplegia and ataxia type cerebral palsy
Answer: d

57. Absolute contraindications to External Cephalic Version in Breechinclude all EXCEPT

a. Oligohydramnios
b. Antepartum hemorrhage
c. Any contraindication to labour
d. Multiple gestation
Answer: a

58. Which of the following is used to deliver an arrested after cominghead in assisted breech delivery of chin to pubis rotated baby ?

a. Scanzoni maneuver
b. Pajot's maneuver
c. Prague maneuver
d. Kristellar maneuver
Answer: c

59. Which is NOT a contraindication to vacuum extraction ?

a. Brow presentation
b. Fetal bleeding disorder or demineralization disorder
c. Previous fetal scalp sampling
d. Less than 34 weeks of gestation
Answer: c

60. All the following are TRUE EXCEPT

a. Third-and fourth-degree lacerations at delivery are associated with anincreased risk of fecal incontinence (OR 2-3)
b. Patients with occult anal sphincter tears are 8 times more likely to have fecalincontinence
c. There is sufficient evidence to support primary elective cesarean delivery for thepurpose of preserving fecal continence
d. Both forceps and vacuum-assisted vaginal delivery significantly increase thisrisk, with vacuum being less traumatic than forceps
Answer: c

61. All the following are TRUE statement about gonadaldifferentiation EXCEPT

a. It now appears that both testis and ovary differentiation require dominantlyacting genes
b. SRY activation of SOX 9 may be all that is necessary to activate other genesimportant to testis development
c. WNT4 and R-Spondin 1(RSPO1) genes team to promote ovary development viarepression of SOX9
d. Ovarian differentiation is considered the "default" pathway of sexdeterminationthe automatic result in the absence of a testis-determining factor
Answer: d

62. All are TRUE statements about Complete Androgen InsensitivityEXCEPT

a. One in three phenotypic sisters of an affected individual may have an XYkaryotype but 40% may not have a family history
b. The normal testes produce normal amounts of AMH and testosterone andabsent spermatogenesis, serum LH levels are increased and the serum FSHusually is in the normal range
c. They present with primary amenorrhea, normal breast development, absent orscant pubic and axillary hair, a short vagina and an absent cervix and uterus
d. Gonadectomy generally is best done before puberty because the overall risk fortumor development is 30%
Answer: d

63. The FALSE statement regarding Congenital Adrenal Hyperplasiais

a. An females, the classic forms of CAH (with and without salt wasting) arecharacterized by genital ambiguity and is most commonly due to 21-hydroxylasedeficiency
b. Two-thirds of patients with 11β-hydroxylase deficiency exhibit hypotension andhypokalemia
c. Females with the non-classical "late-onset" form of 21-hydroxlyased deficiencyhave normal external genitalia and present later, during early adolescence withprecocious puberty or other signs of hyperandrogenism such as hirsutism
d. Diagnosis of 21-hydroxylase deficiency is based on a high serum concentrationof 17-OH Progesterone
Answer: b

64. The FALSE statement about Puberty in humans is

a. "diphasic" pattern of gonadotropin secretion from infancy to puberty resultsprimarily from a high sensitivity to low levels of gonadal steroid feedback
b. central GABA signaling is one of the factors that restrains GnRH neuronalactivity during childhood
c. glutamate signaling may play a role in the resurgence of pulsatile GnRHsecretion at the onset of puberty
d. hypothalamic kisspeptin-GPR54 signaling is a key component of theneurobiologic mechanism that triggers the onset of puberty
Answer: a

65. All are TRUE regarding premature ovarian Insufficiency (POI)EXCEPT

a. In all patients under age 30 with a diagnosis of POI, a karyotype should beobtained
b. Women with POI should be offered testing for FMR1 premutations
c. Women with POI should be screened for antiadrenal antibodies and forantithyroid antibodies
d. Likelihood of achieving pregnancy after diagnosis of POI is about 60-80% anddonor eggs are rarely required for IVF
Answer: d

66. The FALSE statement regarding PolyCystic Ovarian Syndrome(PCOS) is

a. AMH production is increased severalfold in anovulatory PCOS
b. Those with PCOS generally exhibit altered GnRH pulse frequency, increasedserum LH concentrations and low-normal FSH levels
c. Insulin acts synergistically with LH to perpetuate ovarian androgen productionand also inhibits hepatic SHBG production
d. Insulin resistance due to obesity also causes increased leptinsignalling andincreased adiponectin levels, there by decreasing fatty acid oxidation andpromoting lipotoxicity
Answer: d

67. Identify the FALSE statement about Metformin

a. Metformin increases insulin sensitivity up to 20% and decreases fasting glucoseby about 5%
b. Metformin decreases weight and BMI by 3-5%
c. Metformin has no effect on lipolysis and HDL cholesterol
d. Metformin improves the chronic inflammatory state in women withhyperinsulinemia
Answer: c

68. All statements regarding Familial cancers are TRUE EXCEPT

a. about 15-20% of women who develop ovarian cancer have mutations in BRCA1gene
b. Prophylacticsalpingo-oophorectomy reduces the risk of ovarian cancer by about90% and the risk of breast cancer by about 50%
c. Risk-reducing salpingo-oophorectomy is recommended at age 35 or whenchildbearing is complete for patients carrying BRCA1 mutations and by age 40 inBRCA2 carriers
d. The use of combined oral contraceptives is likely to reduce the risk of ovariancancer, but the effect on breast cancer risk is uncertain
Answer: a

69. All are TRUE about Tamoxifen EXCEPT

a. Tamoxifen is selective estrogen receptor modulator, having both estrogenreceptorantagonist and agonist properties, depending on the tissue
b. The incidence of endometrial cancer quadrupled with 5 years of tamoxifentreatment
c. Levonorgestrel intrauterine device (IUD) is not effective to protect theendometrium against hyperplasia and polyps in women using tamoxifen

d. Tamoxifen is associated with an ultrasonographic image that is characterizedby sonolucent changes that are subepithelial in the presence of atrophicepithelium

Answer: c

70. Identify the FALSE statement about Endometrial Hyperplasia

a. Lesions without atypia basically represent only exaggerated forms of persistentproliferative endometrium and are associated with little risk (1-3%) forprogression to adenocarcinoma

b. Atypical endometrial hyperplasia does not often spontaneously regress and hassignificant risk (10-30%) of progression to adenocarcinoma if left untreated

c. There is significant risk (upto 40%) of an unrecognized adenocarcinoma inendometrial hyperplasia with atypia

d. Biopsy is not indicated when the clinical history suggests long-term unopposedestrogen exposure but the endometrial thickness is 5-12 mm

Answer: d

71. Find the FALSE statement regarding HPV induced CIN.

a. HPV-16 infection is a very specific finding and can be found in only 2% ofwomen with normal cervical cytology

b. HPV-18 is more specific than HPV-16 for invasive tumors

c. Metaplasia found at the squamocolumnar junction, begins in the subcolumnarreserve cells

d. As the CIN lesions become more severe, the HPV copy numbers decrease, andthe capsid antigen disappears

Answer: a

72. The sensitivity of cervical cytology testing by Pap Smear for thedetection of CIN 2 or 3 ranges from

a. 60 to 95%

b. 47% to 62%

c. 20-30%

d. 10-15%

Answer: b

73. Cervical conisation is indicated in all EXCEPT

a. ECC histologic findings are positive for CIN 2 or CIN 3

b. Lack of correlation between cytology, biopsy and colposcopy

c. Type I transformation zone

d. Diagnosis of AGC-AIS

Answer: c

74. The following drugs are approved for treatment of GenitourinarySyndrome of Menopause (GSM) EXCEPT

a. Ospemifene

b. 17 beta oestradiol

c. Paroxetine

d. DHEA

Answer: c

75. Following are the duties of a Registered Medical Practitionerunder POCSO Act of India EXCEPT

a. The registered medical practitioner shall submit the report on the condition ofthe child within 48 hrs to the SJPU or local police

b. Provide prophylaxis for identified STD including prophylaxis for HIV andemergency contraception

c. Shall request for legal or magisterial requisition or other documentation priorto rendering such care

d. Options 1) and 3)

Answer: d

76. Using WHO classification for Semen Analysis interpretation,choose the FALSE statement Is

a. The normal lower limit for normal morphology is 4%

b. The normal lower limit for sperm motility is 32%

c. Viability should be at least 58%

d. The normal lower limit for sperm concentration is 39 million/mL

Answer: d

77. Contraindications to using Gonadotropins for ovulation inductionin infertile women include all EXCEPT

a. Uncontrolled thyroid and adrenal dysfunction
b. Hypogonadotropichypogonadism due to space occupying lesions
c. Sex hormone-dependent tumors of the reproductive tract and accecssoryorgans
d. Kallmann syndrome
Answer: d

78. All the following are methods to decrease OHSS EXCEPT

a. HCG trigger
b. GnRH antagonists
c. Invitro oocyte maturation
d. Cabergoline
Answer: a

79. All statements about heterotopic pregnancy are TRUE EXCEPT

a. 1 in 30000 in spontaneous conceptions, as high as 1% with IVF treatment
b. Only 26% of heterotopic cases can be diagnosed with transvaginal US
c. Most often diagnosed in the first 5 to 8 weeks of gestation
d. After treatment of a heterotopic gestation, the overall delivery rate for theintrauterine pregnancy is only 10-20%
Answer: d

80. All the following are independent prognostic variables inendometrial cancer EXCEPT

a. Myometrial invasion
b. Peritoneal cytology
c. Tumor size
d. Lymph node metastasis
Answer: b

81. Find the INCORRECT statement regarding endometrial cancer.

a. Inactivation of the PTEN tumor-suppressor gene is the most common geneticdefect in type I cancers
b. Type I cancers arise from its precursor Endometrial Intraepithelial Carcinoma(EIC)
c. Type II cancers frequently demonstrate alterations in HER2/neu,p53,p16,E-cadherin and loss of LOH
d. Type II endometrial cancer appears to be unrelated to high estrogen levels andoften develops in nonobese women
Answer: b

82. All are TRUE regarding Leiomyosarcoma EXCEPT

a. This malignancy has no relationship with parity
b. A history of prior pelvic radiation can be elicited in about 50% of women withuterine LMS
c. Surgery is the mainstay of treatment for uterine LMS
d. Retroperitoneal lymphatic spread is rare in women with early-stage disease andlymphadenectomy is not associated with a survival advantage
Answer: b

83. All the following are TRUE about TTTS EXCEPT

a. Although growth discordance or growth restriction may be found with TTTS,these per se are not considered diagnostic criteria
b. TTTS is diagnosed in a monochorionicdiamnionic pregnancy when there isoligamnios SVP<2 cm in one sac and polyhydramnios SVP>8 in the other sac
c. Sonography surveillance of pregnancies at risk for TTTS should begin at 16weeks and continue every 2 weeks
d. The discrepancies in amnionic fluid volumes of TTTS are also typically seen inTwin Anaemia Polycythemia Sequence (TAPS)
Answer: d

84. Find the FALSE statement regarding 2018 FIGO staging of cancer cervix.

a. Tumour of size ≥ 2 cm and < 4 cm confined to the cervix is stage IB2
b. Imaging and pathology can be used, where available, to supplement clinicalfindings with respect

to tumor size and extent, in all stages
c. The involvement of lymph nodes are not part of staging
d. The lateral extent of the lesion is no longer considered
Answer: c

85. The boundaries of paravesical space include all EXCEPT

a. The obliterated umbilical artery running along the bladder medially
b. The obturator internus muscle along the pelvic sidewall laterally
c. The uterosacral ligament posteriorly
d. The pubic symphysis anteriorly
Answer: c

86. All are TRUE about antiphospholipid antibody syndrome EXCEPT

a. Asherson syndrome is a rapidly progressive thromboembolic disorder due to acytokine storm seen in antiphospolipid antibody syndrome
b. Approximately 60 percent of patients with APS have a positive lupusanticoagulant LAC assay alone
c. Heparin binds to beta 2 glycoprotein I and prevents binding of anticardiolipinandanti-beta 2 glycoprotein I antibodies to the syncytiotrophoblasts
d. Treatment using aspirin, anticoagulation and close monitoring has increasedlive birth rates to more than 70 percent in women with APS
Answer: b

87. All are TRUE about management of obstetric haemorrhageEXCEPT

a. The most important mechanism of action with internal iliac artery ligation is an85-percent reduction in pulse pressure in those arteries distal to the ligation
b. ROTEM or TEG cannot diagnose coagulopathies stemming from plateletdysfunction or anti platelet drugs
c. Each single-donor apheresis six-unit bag raises the platelet count byapproximately 5000/L
d. Dilutional coagulopathy that is clinically indistinguishable from DIC is the mostfrequent coagulation defect found with blood loss and multiple transfusions
Answer: c

88. All are TRUE about USS features of Placenta Accreta Spectrum(PAS) EXCEPT

a. loss of the normal hypoechoicretroplacentalzone between the placenta anduterus
b. placental vascular lacunae or lakes
c. distance between the uterine serosa-bladder wall interface and theretroplacental vessels measures < 10 mm
d. placental bulging into the posterior bladder wall
Answer: c

89. USS has a sensitivity of _____________ in suspected abruptioplacenta.

a. 24%
b. 54%
c. 81%
d. 93%
Answer: a

90. All are TRUE about COVID-19 in pregnancy EXCEPT

a. It is associated with an almost three times greater risk of preterm birth (17%)
b. Majority of pregnant women (74%) may be asymptomatic
c. ICU admissions are not more common in pregnant women compared tononpregnant women of the same age
d. Risk factors associated with hospital admissions include older age, obesity,diabetes and hypertension
Answer: c

91. All are TRUE regarding Fetomaternal unit in pregnancy EXCEPT

a. Progesterone production by the placenta is largely independent of the quantityof precursor available, the utero-placental perfusion and fetal well-being
b. There is a 17 alpha hydroxylase enzyme block in the fetus and placenta has verylittle 3 beta hydroxyl steroid dehydrogenase activity
c. Cholesterol and pregnenolone are obtained mainly from the maternalbloodstream for placental progesterone synthesis

d. In human syncytiotrophoblast, estradiol increases progesterone production bymeans of an increase in LDL uptake
Answer: b

92. All are TRUE statements about Corpus luteum of PregnancyEXCEPT
a. Progesterone is largely produced by the corpus luteum until about 10 weeks ofgestation
b. Pulsatile luteinizing hormone (LH) and human chorionic gonadotropin (hCG)from the implanting pregnancy stimulate progesterone production by the corpusluteum
c. In the luteal phase of conception cycles, progesterone concentrations increasefrom about 1-2 mg/mL on the day of the LH surge to a plateau of approximately10-35 mg/mL
d. The transitional luteo-placental shift takes place between the 10□ h week and12□ h week
Answer: d

93. The FALSE statement regarding the glycoprotein hormoneHuman Chorionic Gonadotropin (HCG) is
a. A maximal level of about 100,000 IU/L in the maternal circulation is reached at8-10 weeks of gestation
b. Long half-life of hCG (48 hours) is due mainly to the greater amino acidcontent of beta subunit
c. Hyperglycosylated hCG is the major circulating form of hCG regulatingtrophoblastic invasion in the first weeks of normal pregnancies
d. β-hCG can be detected in maternal blood about the eighth day after ovulationor one day after implantation
Answer: b

94. Find out the FALSE statement regarding human parturition
a. The initiating step in the sequence of events leading to parturition could beanincrease in fetal ACTH and cortisol secretion and an increase in placental CRH
b. There is a definite decline in peripheral blood levels of progesterone prior toparturition and not just a functional withdrawal
c. An increase in estrogen levels in maternal blood begins at 34-35 weeks
d. The activity of 15-hydroxyprostaglandin dehydrogenase decreases in themyometrium and the chorion during labor and causes increase in prostaglandinsassociated with parturition
Answer: b

95. All the following statements about fetal lung surfactant are TRUEEXCEPT
a. Phosphatidylcholine (lecithin) and phosphatidylglycerol (PG) are present inonly small concentrations until the last 5 weeks of pregnancy
b. At 20-22 weeks of pregnancy, a less stable and less active lecithin, palmitoyl-myristoyl lecithin, is formed
c. At about the 30□ h week of gestation, there is a sudden surge of dipalmitoyllecithin, the major surfactant lecithin
d. The Sphingomyelin concentration of amniotic fluid changes relatively littlethroughout pregnancy and prior to 34 weeks, the Lecithin : Sphingomyelin L/Sratio is approximately 1 : 1
Answer: c

96. STRAW stage-3a is characterized by
a. menstrual cycles are relatively unchanged, the serum levels of FSH are low,AMH and inhibin B are low
b. menstrual cycles become shorter, FSH increases, while AMH, AFC and inhibinB declines
c. periods of amenorrhea lasting greater than or equal to 60 days, FSH level inmenopausal range, vasomotor symptoms such as hot flushes
d. undetectable AMH, Inhibin and occasional antral follicle
Answer: b

97. The FALSE statement regarding Menopausal Hormone Therapy(MHT/HRT) is
a. Continuous, combined estrogen-progestin regimens of HRT has more risk forendometrial cancer than long-term sequential regimens
b. Ospemifene is given orally for the treatment of vulvar and vaginal atrophy
c. Bazedoxifene combined with conjugated estrogens is effective for hot flushesand vaginal atrophy, prevents bone loss and does not stimulate the endometriumor cause breast tenderness
d. The use of tibolone in women with a history of breast cancer remains relativelycontraindicated
Answer: a

98. All the statements about Emergency Contraception are TRUEEXCEPT
a. Copper IUD can be used anytime during the preovulatory phase of themenstrual cycle and upto 8 days after ovulation
b. Ulipristal acetate is slightly more effective than the single 1.5-mg dose oflevonorgestrel when used within 120 hours
c. Mifepristone prevents about 80-85% of expected pregnancies and has the sameefficacy and side effects as levonorgestrel method
d. Treatment with Levonorgestrel acts primarily by preventing or delayingovulation and by preventing fertilization
Answer: a
99. The FALSE statement about etonogestrel Implant (Nexplanon) is
a. Inhibits ovulation by preventing LH surge and failure rate is 0.01%
b. Implants have an immediate contraceptive effect when inserted within the first7 days of a menstrual cycle
c. Implants should not be inserted immediate postpartum
d. It is absolutely contraindicated in women with active thromboembolic diseaseor known breast cancer
Answer: c
100. All the statements about reproductive ageing are TRUE EXCEPT
a. Age related Oocyte aneuploidy results primarily from premature separation ofsister chromatids during meiosis I or from whole chromosome nondisjunctionduring meiosis II
b. Miscarriage riks and the prevalence of aneuploidy oocytes are relatively lowand change little until approximately age 35
c. Live birth rates in donor egg IVF cycles relate to the age of the donor, not theage of the recipient
d. Aging itself is thought to be a significant factor influencing uterine endometrialresponse to steroids and receptivity
Answer: d

Printed by Libri Plureos GmbH in Hamburg,
Germany